NOT–FOR–PROFIT
BUDGETING
AND FINANCIAL
MANAGEMENT

NOT-FOR-PROFIT BUDGETING AND FINANCIAL MANAGEMENT

EDWARD J. McMILLAN, CPA, CAE

WILEY

John Wiley & Sons, Inc.

Other books by Edward J. McMillan:
Model Policies and Procedures for Not-for-Profit Organizations
Not-for-Profit Accounting, Tax, and Reporting Requirements

The second edition of this book was titled *Budgeting and Financial Management Handbook for Not-for-Profit Organizations.*

This book is printed on acid-free paper. ∞

Copyright © 2003 by John Wiley & Sons, Inc. All rights reserved.

Published by John Wiley & Sons, Inc., Hoboken, New Jersey
Published simultaneously in Canada

For general information on our other products and services, or technical support, please contact our Customer Care Department within the United States at 800-762-2974, outside the United States at 317-572-3993 or fax 317-572-4002.

Wiley also publishes its books in a variety of electronic formats. Some content that appears in print may not be available in electronic books.

For more information about Wiley products, visit our web site at www.wiley.com.

Library of Congress Cataloging-in-Publication Data:

McMillan, Edward J., 1949–
   Not-for-profit budgeting and financial management / Edward J. McMillan.—3rd ed., rev. and expanded.
      p. cm.
"The second edition of this book was titled Budgeting and financial management handbook for not-for-profit organizations"—T.p. verso.
Includes bibliographical references and index.
   ISBN 0-471-45314-5 (pbk. : alk. paper)
   1. Nonprofit organizations—Finance.   2. Nonprofit organizations—Accounting.   3. Corporations—Finance.
4. Corporations—Accounting.   5. Budget in business.   I. McMillan, Edward J., 1949– Budgeting and financial management handbook for not-for-profit organizations.   II. Title.
   HG4027.65.M364 2003
   658.15—dc21

                                                                                    2003050165

Printed in the United States of America

10 9 8 7 6 5 4 3 2 1

To my mother,
Audrey Elizabeth McMillan

About the Author

Edward J. McMillan, CPA, CAE, has spent his entire career in not-for-profit financial management. He has served as the controller of the national office of the Associated Builders and Contractors and as the finance and membership director of the American Correctional Association. In 1993, McMillan was appointed faculty chair for finance for the United States Chamber of Commerce's Institutes for Organization Management program.

McMillan has written several books on not-for-profit financial management. His publishers include the American Society of Association Executives, McGraw-Hill, the U.S. Chamber of Commerce, and the American Chamber of Commerce.

McMillan now concentrates solely on speaking, writing, and consulting on financial management topics for associations and chambers of commerce. He lives near Annapolis, Maryland. In his free time, he enjoys coaching youth sports and motocross racing. You may contact McMillan at P.O. Box 771, Forest Hill, MD 21050; phone/fax: (410) 893-2308; e-mail: emcmillan@sprintmail.com. Also see his Web site at www.nonprofitguru.com.

Contents

List of Exhibits

Preface

Typically, not-for-profit organizations view the budget process as an annual exercise in drudgery, tying up valuable staff time that could have been spent on other activities. It doesn't have to be that way!

This handbook will apprise you of a new concept in budgeting that is easy to implement, is easy to monitor, will significantly reduce staff time spent on budgeting, and will ensure true fiscal accountability. The method is called continuous budgeting.

You should review this handbook in its entirety before you implement your financial management system. The processes and forms herein are interdependent and must be understood by management before the advantages of this system can be realized. This handbook was written as a guide to help managers customize the forms and procedures described herein for use in their own organizations.

This book was not written as a reference manual on taxes, depreciation, capitalization procedures, and other technical areas. There are other sources for that information. This handbook was written in a nontechnical, understandable, how-to language and format. The program allows management to direct and control the organization rather than be controlled by an outdated, cumbersome, and generally inaccurate budget and financial management system.

Edward J. McMillan, CPA, CAE
September 2003

NOT-FOR-PROFIT BUDGETING AND FINANCIAL MANAGEMENT

Basic Accounting and Financial Operations

A WELL-RUN ORGANIZATION must have an efficient financial operation in place to implement an effective budgeting program. An effective financial operation should integrate the following:

➤ Accurate financial data

➤ Understandable financial statements that meet the organization's needs

➤ Timely financial statements

➤ Actual versus budget figures for the period presented

➤ An annual audit by an independent certified public accountant (CPA) firm

Accurate Financial Data

Financial statements are prepared by one of two accounting methods:

➤ Cash basis of accounting—recognizes revenues when cash is received and expenses when cash is disbursed.

➤ Accrual basis of accounting—recognizes revenues when they are earned and expenses when they are incurred. The actual receipt and disbursement of cash generally does not result in recognizing revenues and expenses. Accrual accounting also attempts to match revenues with corresponding expenses in the proper accounting period.

Unless an organization is very small or is a true cash business, the accrual method of accounting results in much more accurate and meaningful financial statements than the cash basis does. Accrual-based financial statements are more difficult to prepare, but the resulting accuracy is crucial to good budgeting.

Understandable Financial Statements

Financial statements should be constructed to provide management with what it needs to effectively control the organization. The statements should compare actual versus budget data for both the current month and the year to date. They should be understandable to nonaccounting management and easy to interpret. In addition, the statements should be streamlined, relatively brief, and not bogged down with unnecessary detail that will frustrate the reader.

Timely Financial Statements

Internal financial statements should be prepared and distributed monthly and within 10 business days after the close of the prior month. When the statements are prepared other than monthly and it takes longer than 10 days to prepare and distribute them, management's ability to take well-thought-out action to correct problems diminishes. Rather, decisions are likely to be based on old data, problems may worsen, and valuable time that could have been used to correct the problem will have been lost.

Internal financial statements should include, at a minimum, the two primary financial statements:

➢ The Statement of Financial Position (the balance sheet)

➢ The Statement of Activity (the income statement)

Statement of Financial Position

The Statement of Financial Position shows the overall financial health of an organization at a point in time by comparing the organization's assets, liabilities, and net assets. It usually does not reflect actual versus budget goals. The Statement of Financial Position illustrates an organization's solvency and cash position but does not reflect profitability. A sample Statement of Financial Position for a typical not-for-profit organization is shown in Exhibit 1.1.

Statement of Activity

The Statement of Activity shows the profitability of an organization for a specific period by comparing revenues and expenses. It does not reflect the organization's solvency. The Statement of Activity illustrates both current-month and year-to-date figures to help management understand the financial condition of the organization. It also serves as a budgeting tool. A sample Statement of Activity for a typical not-for-profit organization is shown in Exhibit 1.2.

EXHIBIT 1.1

Sample Statement of Financial Position

**Statement of Financial Position
(Balance Sheet)
February 28, 20X0**

ASSETS

CURRENT ASSETS

Cash and Cash Equivalents	Checking Accounts	$116,786	
	Savings Accounts	150,016	
	Certificates of Deposit	200,000	$466,802
Accounts Receivable		$77,171	
Less Allowance for Doubtful Accounts		(10,000)	67,171
Prepaid Expenses			5,095
Inventory			10,714
Total Current Assets			549,782

FURNITURE, EQUIPMENT, AND IMPROVEMENTS

Building and Land	$511,992	
Furniture and Equipment	249,776	
Leasehold Improvements	9,097	
Less Accumulated Depreciation and Amortization	(105,750)	
Total Furniture, Equipment, and Improvements		665,115

RESTRICTED ASSETS

Temporarily Restricted	$103,895	
Permanently Restricted	200,000	
Total Restricted Assets		303,895

TOTAL ASSETS	**$1,518,792**

LIABILITIES AND NET ASSETS

CURRENT LIABILITIES

Accounts Payable	$111,458	
Accrued Payroll	2,098	
Total Current Liabilities		$113,556

LONG-TERM LIABILITIES

Notes Payable	$30,904	
Mortgage Payable	304,789	
Total Long-Term Liabilities		335,693

DEFERRED INCOME

Dues	$104,904	
Conferences	23,333	
Advertising	10,148	
Total Deferred Income		138,385

NET ASSETS

Unrestricted Net Assets	$627,263	
Temporarily Restricted Net Assets	103,895	
Permanently Restricted Net Assets	200,000	
Total Net Assets		931,158

TOTAL LIABILITIES AND NET ASSETS	**$1,518,792**

EXHIBIT 1.2

Sample Statement of Activity

Statement of Activity
(Income Statement)
For the Two-Month Period Ended February 28, 20X0

	Current Month		Year to Date	
Revenues				
Dues		$278,050		$576,398
Publication Sales	$51,360		$107,834	
Less Cost of Goods Sold	(15,780)	35,580	(38,970)	68,864
Advertising		36,480		77,250
Interest		2,141		4,359
Conference				
Registration	$58,888		$130,780	
Exhibits	10,700	69,588	22,700	153,480
Other		3,903		7,240
Total Revenues		$425,742		$887,591
Expenses				
Salaries		$283,290		$405,760
Fringe Benefits		39,404		45,790
Payroll Taxes		26,426		33,391
Printing		46,644		62,764
Travel		5,043		25,471
Rent		30,000		60,000
Utilities		2,705		4,848
Supplies		1,002		2,052
Telephone		1,303		12,205
Insurance		1,025		2,050
Interest		13,400		26,800
Other Taxes		10,000		11,042
Depreciation		2,045		4,090
Amortization		253		506
Postage		8,309		18,098
Maintenance Contracts		1,304		2,608
Lease Contracts		2,052		4,104
Independent Contractors		8,340		16,690
Miscellaneous		1,566		3,203
Total Expenses		$484,111		$741,472
Increase in Unrestricted				
Net Assets		($58,369)		$146,139

Annual Audit

An effective budget is based on accurate financial data. Management can ensure records are accurate by having the records audited by an independent CPA firm. The audit process requires the CPA firm to advise and make recommendations to management as to weaknesses and problems with accounting systems. Management may not be aware of these problems, and the audit will afford an opportunity to correct deficiencies. In addition, an audit will include an internal control survey and a management letter:

> An internal control survey is designed to expose weaknesses surrounding the safeguarding of cash and other assets and is an annual requirement of a CPA's auditing standards.

> A management letter is the vehicle CPA firms use to alert management to inefficiencies that come to light during the audit. The management letter also includes recommendations for improvement.

Organizations that cannot afford a full audit should at least consider a less costly review or compilation.

CHAPTER 2

Effective Use of Footnotes and Financial Ratio Calculations for the Statement of Financial Position

Footnotes

WHILE THE STATEMENTS of Activity are relatively easy to understand, presenting and explaining the Statement of Financial Position to a primarily nonfinancial board of directors can be difficult.

With this in mind, consider using footnotes to thoroughly detail every asset and liability account. It may be somewhat time consuming to prepare a footnoted statement the first time, but once this process is completed initially, subsequent presentations will be a very simple matter, as most of the account descriptions will not change from month to month.

Also, remember that there are going to be questions concerning any financial statement presentation and if the questions are answered before they are asked, it will appear that the statements have been well thought out and researched.

A footnoted Statement of Financial Position may appear as in Exhibit 2.1.

EXHIBIT 2.1

Sample Statement of Financial Position

Statement of Financial Position
(Balance Sheet)
February 28, 20X0

ASSETS

CURRENT ASSETS

[1]Unrestricted Cash and

Cash Equivalents	[2]Checking Accounts	$116,786	
	[3]Savings Accounts	150,016	
	[4]Certificates of Deposit	200,000	$466,802
[5]Accounts Receivable		$77,171	
[6]Less Allowance for Doubtful Accounts		(10,000)	67,171
[7]Prepaid Expenses			5,095
[8]Inventory			10,714

Total Current Assets $549,782

FURNITURE, EQUIPMENT, AND IMPROVEMENTS

[9]Building and Land	$511,992	
[10]Furniture and Equipment	249,776	
[11]Leasehold Improvements	9,097	770,865
[12]Less Accumulated Depreciation and Amortization		(105,750)

[13]Total Furniture, Equipment, and Improvements   665,115

[14]RESTRICTED ASSETS

[15]Temporarily Restricted	$103,895
[16]Permanently Restricted	200,000

Total Restricted Assets   303,895

TOTAL ASSETS $1,518,792

LIABILITIES AND NET ASSETS

[17]CURRENT LIABILITIES

[18]Accounts Payable	$61,458
[19]Accrued Payroll	2,098
[20]Current Portion of Mortgages and Notes	50,000

Total Current Liabilities $113,556

EXHIBIT 2.1 *(Continued)*		
[21]LONG-TERM LIABILITIES		
[22]Notes Payable	$30,904	
[23]Mortgage Payable	304,789	
Total Long-Term Liabilities		335,693
[24]DEFERRED INCOME		
[25]Dues	$104,904	
[26]Conferences	23,333	
[27]Advertising	10,148	
Total Deferred Income		138,385
[28]NET ASSETS		
[29]Unrestricted Net Assets	$627,263	
[30]Temporarily Restricted Net Assets	103,895	
[31]Permanently Restricted Net Assets	200,000	
Total Net Assets		931,158
TOTAL LIABILITIES AND NET ASSETS		$1,518,792

Footnotes Explained

[1]Unrestricted check and cash equivalents are always listed first on a properly prepared Statement of Financial Position. Cash equivalents are accounts that can be converted into cash quickly (irrespective of premature conversion penalties and the like) such as certificates of deposit (CDs). Restricted cash is listed separately (in proximity with fixed assets) so as not to mislead financial ratio computations.

[2]The organization currently has a disbursing account and a payroll checking account at (bank name) with current balances totaling $116,786. Both are money market accounts presently earning an interest rate of _____%.

[3]The organization has a savings account at (bank name) currently earning _____% interest with a current available balance of $150,016. There is no maturity date, so withdrawals are not penalized.

[4]The organization has one CD at (bank name) in the amount of $100,000 that is credited with an interest rate of _____% and matures on (date), with a premature withdrawal penalty of _____%.

Additionally, the organization has a second CD at (bank name) also in the amount of $100,000 that is credited with an interest rate of _____%, matures on (date), and has a premature withdrawal penalty of _____%.

[5]Accounts receivable are monies legally owed to the organization by exhibitors, advertisers, book purchasers, and so forth. Current account receivable balances are as follows:

Advertisers	$20,000
Exhibitors	20,000
Book purchasers	26,486
Misc.	10,685
Total	$77,171

Important: As accounts receivable are technically *legal* obligations, the organization has adopted a policy whereby amounts billed to members for *dues* are not reflected on the Statement of Financial Position. As of the date of the statement, the total amount of billed but unpaid dues is $_____ and, based on the historical retention rate, the organization fully expects to receive $_____ of this amount.

EXHIBIT 2.1 *(Continued)*

[6]Based on past history, the organization has set up a realistic bad debt allowance of $10,000 on the present level of non-dues accounts receivable.

[7]Prepaid expenses are amounts the organization has expended for which it will receive a future benefit. The organization's accounting policy states that these amounts will be reclassified as line-item expenses in the month the benefit is realized. A schedule of prepaid expenses and expense reclassification dates are as follows:

Item	Amount	Reclassification Date
Deposit on Convention Hotel	$5,095	Month, Year

[8]Inventory values are recorded at the organization's *cost* using the average-cost method of valuation for merchandise held for sale for member and nonmember purchases.
Current level of inventory is:

Item	Amount
Books	$7,700
Clothing	3,014
Total	$10,714

[9]Accounting regulations state that the organization's building, plus improvements, must be recorded in this financial statement at its *historical cost* and *not* its current market value.
A history of the building value is as follows:

	Amount	Date
Original purchase price of land	$100,000	(date)
Original purchase price of building	300,000	(date)
Improvement	50,000	(date)
Improvement	61,992	(date)
Total cost basis	$511,992	

Note: The land and building have a real estate tax assessed value of $750,000. Additionally, the real estate was appraised on (month/year) and the appraisal value was $850,000.

[10]Furniture and equipment are also recorded in the financial statement at a historical cost of $249,776, and no appraisal value is available.

[11]Leasehold improvements of $9,097 are expenses realized to install a security alarm at the rented warehouse where books and clothing held for resale are stored off site.

[12]The organization policy is to depreciate and amortize assets using the straight-line method according to the following schedule:

Item	Time Period
Building	30 years
Land	Nondepreciable asset
Furniture	10 years
Electronic assets	3 years
Leasehold improvements	Lease period remaining

[13]The net value (cost less depreciation and amortization) is also called the *book value* of capitalized assets, and is as follows:

Item	Cost	Accumulated Depreciation and Amortization	Book Value
Land and building	$511,992	$(50,000)	$461,992
Furniture and equipment	249,776	(50,000)	199,776
Leasehold improvements	9,097	(5,750)	3,347
Totals	$770,865	$(105,750)	$665,115

[14]Accounting statements for not-for-profit organizations specify that assets held by the organizations that have been restricted by the donors be presented in proximity with fixed assets on the Statement of Financial Position. With this in

EXHIBIT 2.1 *(Continued)*

mind, our independent auditors note these accounts as the last assets presented on audited financial statements, and the organization follows this practice for consistency and also so as to not result in misleading financial ratio computations. *Note:* The organization's restricted funds are *not* commingled with unrestricted funds.

[15]Temporarily restricted net assets will eventually be spent for the purpose of the restriction:

Item	Amount
Scholarship A	$53,895
Scholarship B	50,000
Total	$103,895

These accounts are presently in the form of two savings accounts, both at (bank name) and both receiving a current interest rate of return of _____%. Interest is also used for scholarships.

[16]The organization received an endowment in the amount of $200,000 from (donor) on (date). The principal (corpus) must be kept in perpetuity and the interest received is unrestricted revenue. The $200,000 is presently in the form of a CD at (bank name) earning an interest rate of _____% and matures on (date).
Interest earned on the CD is deposited directly into the organization's unrestricted savings account (see footnote #3) by the bank.

[17]Current liabilities are amounts legally owed by the organization to vendors, banks, and so forth, within 12 months of the date of the statement.

[18]Accounts payable are legal obligations owed to vendors for goods and services provided and currently total $61,458. The organization's policy with vendors is such that invoices will be paid within 30 days of the receipt of the invoices. The organization also has a policy whereby it takes advantage of prompt payment discounts when offered.

[19]The organization employs a biweekly payroll system whereby all employees are paid every other Friday. As of the date of this statement, employees worked (#) days in (month) for a liability of ($_____) that was paid to employees on (date).

[20]Amounts due to be paid on the mortgage and notes payable over the next 12 succeeding months are as follows:

Item	Amount
Mortgage on building	$40,000
Note on data processing system	10,000
Total	$50,000

[21]Long-term debt is for amounts owed on mortgages and notes *excluding* the next 12 months' payments. The current portion of long-term debt is classified with current liabilities.

[22]The organization borrowed funds to finance the data processing system in the form of a secured note. The loan details are as follows:

Original loan amount	$(amount)
Lending institution	(bank)
Date of loan	(date)
Length of loan	(years)
Interest rate	_____%
Debt service	$_____/month
Payoff date	(date)

[23]The organization borrowed funds to finance the building and land in the form of a mortgage. The mortgage details are as follows:

Original mortgage amount	$(amount)
Lending institution	(bank)
Date of loan	(date)
Length of loan	(years)
Interest rate	_____%
Debt service	$_____/month
Payoff date	(date)

EXHIBIT 2.1 *(Continued)*

[24]Deferred income is funds the organization has received for which it owes a future service. These amounts will be reclassified as revenues in the month the service is provided.

[25]The organization's accounting policy with regard to dues is such that one-twelfth ($\frac{1}{12}$) of dues received each month is recorded as dues revenue in the month received and the remaining dues are deferred. Deferred dues are reclassified as dues revenue over the next 11 months.

[26]Deferred conference revenues are down payments received from exhibitors for the annual conference. These funds will be reclassified as exhibitor revenues after the conference has been held in (month/year).
The reason these monies are considered liabilities is that, in the event the conference is not held, the deposits would have to be refunded to the exhibitors.

[27]Deferred advertising revenues are funds the organization has received in February from advertisers for the March issue of the magazine. These amounts will be reclassified as advertising revenue in March, when the magazine has been printed.

[28]The net assets section of this statement is unique to not-for-profit organizations and represents the organization's equity section.

[29]Unrestricted net assets are similar to the retained earnings account appearing on the financial statements of commercial organizations in that they represent the net profit of the organization since it has been in existence.
Unrestricted net assets are also the organization's theoretical book-value net worth.

[30]Temporarily restricted net assets represent the liability to fund scholarships addressed in footnote #15. As scholarships are awarded, the balances in both the scholarship cash account and the liability account decline.

[31]Permanently restricted net assets represent the liability to hold the endowment noted in footnote #16 in perpetuity.

Important Financial Ratios
Equity Computations
As of February 28, 20X0

Current Ratio:
This ratio is computed by comparing total current assets to total current liabilities:

549:113 (in thousands)

Acid Test Ratio:
This ratio is computed by comparing cash and cash equivalents *only* to current liabilities:

466:113 (in thousands)

Land and Building Equity

Cost Basis:

Historical cost and improvements	$511,992
Mortgage principal balance, (month/year)	−344,789
Equity, cost basis	$167,203

Appraisal Basis:

Value on last appraisal	$850,000
Mortgage principal balance (month/year)	−344,203
Equity, appraisal basis	$505,797

CHAPTER 3

Controllable and Uncontrollable Expenses

A KEY TO BUDGETING and fiscal accountability is to separate controllable from uncontrollable expenses and to hold managers of not-for-profit organizations accountable for expenses under their direct control only. Although individual departments should be credited and charged for all applicable revenues and expenses, managers of these departments should be held responsible for line items under their direct control only.

Even in larger organizations, department managers control a few line items. Examples may include the following:

➢ Salaries

➢ Travel

➢ Printing

➢ Postage

➢ Supplies

➢ Telephone

➢ Independent contractors

➢ Miscellaneous expenses

Many line items will be completely out of a department manager's control, and these managers should not be held accountable for these items. Examples of uncontrollable line-item expenses may include the following:

➢ Fringe benefits

➢ Payroll taxes

➢ Other taxes

➢ Rent

➢ Utilities

➢ Insurance

➢ Interest expense

➢ Depreciation

➢ Amortization

➢ Maintenance contracts

➢ Lease contracts

Controllability should be considered in the design of internal financial statements that will be used by management.

The Statement of Activity presented in Exhibit 1.2 could be revised to break down expenses into controllable expenses and uncontrollable expenses and may appear as shown in Exhibit 3.1.

Internal financial statements are starting to become more sophisticated than a simple Statement of Activity. Although the statements still do not include budget figures, they are moving in the direction of providing management with customized, understandable information that meets the needs of organizations.

EXHIBIT 3.1

Sample Statement of Activity Listing Controllable and Uncontrollable Expenses

Statement of Activity
(Income Statement)
For the Two-Month Period Ended February 28, 20X0

	Current Month		Year to Date	
Revenues				
Dues		$278,050		$576,398
Publication Sales	$51,360		$107,834	
Less Cost of Goods	(15,780)	35,580	(38,950)	68,884
Advertising		36,480		77,250
Interest		2,141		4,359
Conference				
Registrations	$58,888		$130,780	
Exhibits	10,700	69,588	22,700	153,480
Other		3,903		7,240
Total Revenues		$425,742		$887,611
Expenses				
Controllable Expenses				
Salaries		$283,290		$405,760
Travel		5,043		25,471
Printing		46,644		62,764
Postage		8,309		18,098
Independent Contractors		8,340		16,690
Supplies		1,002		2,052
Telephone		1,303		12,205
Miscellaneous		1,566		3,203
Subtotal		$355,497		$546,243
Uncontrollable Expenses				
Fringe Benefits		$39,404		$45,790
Payroll Taxes		26,426		33,391
Other Taxes		10,000		11,042
Rent		30,000		60,000
Utilities		2,705		4,848
Insurance		1,025		2,050
Interest		13,400		26,800
Depreciation		2,045		4,090
Amortization		253		506
Maintenance Contracts		1,304		2,608
Lease Contracts		2,052		4,104
Subtotal		$128,614		$195,229
Total Expenses		$484,111		$741,472
Increase in Unrestricted Net Assets (Profit)		($58,369)		$146,139

CHAPTER 4

Controllable, Semi-Controllable, and Fixed Expenses

THE STATEMENT OF ACTIVITY illustrated in Exhibit 1.2 was modified in Exhibit 3.1 to distinguish controllable from uncontrollable expenses. In this chapter, the statement is further modified by subdividing expenses into three categories: controllable, semi-controllable, and fixed.

Controllable Expenses

Controllable expenses are discretionary; they can be increased or decreased by management decisions. For example, salary expenses can be reduced by layoffs, and travel expenses can be curtailed by cancelling trips. Truly controllable expenses may include the following:

➢ Salaries

➢ Travel

➢ Printing

➢ Postage

➢ Supplies

➢ Telephone

➢ Miscellaneous

➢ Independent contractors

Controllable expenses should be separated from semi-controllable and fixed expenses on the Statement of Activity for management, budgeting, and fiscal accountability purposes.

Semi-Controllable Expenses

Some expenses may appear to be uncontrollable but can be controlled to a certain degree. These belong in a separate category on the Statement of Activity called "Semi-Controllable Expenses." Payroll taxes are a semi-controllable expense. Although the assessment of payroll taxes is a function of government, payroll taxes are considered semi-controllable because they are directly related to salaries. If salaries are decreased, payroll taxes decrease accordingly. Examples of semi-controllable expenses include the following:

➢ Fringe benefits

➢ Payroll taxes

➢ Other taxes

➢ Utilities

➢ Insurance

Fixed Expenses

Some expenses are not only uncontrollable, but also unchangeable or fixed. Fixed expenses are the third category of expenses. Fixed expenses are a result of a prior-year contractual agreement (such as a lease on a building) or a prior-year transaction that affects the current year (such as depreciation on capital equipment purchased in a prior year). Examples of fixed expenses include the following:

➢ Rent

➢ Lease contracts

➢ Depreciation

➢ Interest on notes and mortgages

➢ Maintenance contracts

➢ Amortization

As with controllable and semi-controllable expenses, fixed expenses should be accounted for separately on the Statement of Activity.

The Statement of Activity modified in Exhibit 3.1 would be further modified and may appear as shown in Exhibit 4.1.

EXHIBIT 4.1

Sample Statement of Activity Listing Controllable, Semi-Controllable, and Fixed Expenses

Statement of Activity
(Income Statement)
For the Two-Month Period Ended February 28, 20X0

	Current Month		Year to Date	
Revenues				
Dues		$278,050		$576,398
Publication Sales	$51,360		$107,834	
Less Cost of Goods Sold	(15,780)	35,580	(38,950)	68,884
Advertising		36,480		77,250
Interest		2,141		4,359
Conference				
Registrations	$58,888		$130,780	
Exhibits	10,700	69,588	22,700	153,480
Other		3,903		7,240
Total Revenues		$425,742		$887,611
Expenses				
Controllable Expenses				
Salaries		$283,290		$405,760
Travel		5,043		25,471
Printing		46,644		62,764
Postage		8,309		18,098
Supplies		1,002		2,052
Telephone		1,303		12,205
Independent Contractors		8,340		16,690
Miscellaneous		1,566		3,203
Subtotal		$355,497		$546,243
Semi-Controllable Expenses				
Fringe Benefits		$39,404		$45,790
Payroll Taxes		26,426		33,391
Other Taxes		10,000		11,042
Utilities		2,705		4,848
Insurance		1,025		2,050
Subtotal		$79,560		$97,121
Fixed Expenses				
Rent		$30,000		$60,000
Interest		13,400		26,800
Lease Contracts		2,052		4,104
Maintenance Contracts		1,304		2,608
Depreciation		2,045		4,090
Amortization		253		506
Subtotal		$49,054		$98,108
Total Expenses		$484,111		$741,472
Increase in Unrestricted Net Assets (Profit)		($58,369)		$146,139

CHAPTER 5

Noncash Expenses

A FINAL CATEGORY of expenses that may be considered is noncash expenses. Non-financial reviewers of financial statements often have difficulty understanding expenses that do not involve the use of cash in the current accounting period.

When an organization purchases an asset that is capitalized (recorded on the Statement of Financial Position as an asset rather than on the Statement of Activity as an expense), the *cash* is expended at the time of purchase and not gradually over the life of the asset.

Typical noncash expense line items for a not-for-profit organization may be depreciation or amortization.

A revised Statement of Activity (see Exhibit 5.1) now separates expenses into four categories:

➢ Controllable expenses

➢ Semi-controllable expenses

➢ Fixed expenses

➢ Noncash expenses

EXHIBIT 5.1

Sample Statement of Activity Listing Controllable, Semi-Controllable, Fixed, and Noncash Expenses

Statement of Activity
(Income Statement)
For the Two-Month Period Ended February 28, 20X0

	Current Month		Year to Date	
Revenues				
Dues		$278,050		$576,398
Publication Sales	$51,360		$107,834	
Less Cost of Goods Sold	(15,780)	35,580	(38,950)	68,884
Advertising		36,480		77,250
Interest		2,141		4,359
Conference				
Registrations	$58,888		$130,780	
Exhibits	10,700	69,588	22,700	153,480
Other		3,903		7,240
Total Revenues		$425,742		$887,611
Expenses				
Controllable Expenses				
Salaries		$283,290		$405,760
Travel		5,043		25,471
Printing		46,644		62,764
Postage		8,309		18,098
Supplies		1,002		2,052
Telephone		1,303		12,205
Independent Contractors		8,340		16,690
Miscellaneous		1,566		3,203
Subtotal		$355,497		$546,243
Semi-Controllable Expenses				
Fringe Benefits		$39,404		$45,790
Payroll Taxes		26,426		33,391
Other Taxes		10,000		11,042
Utilities		2,705		4,848
Insurance		1,025		2,050
Subtotal		$79,560		$97,121

EXHIBIT 5.1 *(Continued)*

	Current Month	Year to Date
Fixed Expenses		
Rent	$30,000	$60,000
Interest	13,400	26,800
Lease Contracts	2,052	4,104
Maintenance Contracts	1,304	2,608
Subtotal	$46,756	$93,512
Total Expenses Before		
Noncash Expenses	$481,813	$736,876
Increase in Unrestricted Net Assets		
Before Noncash Expenses	($56,071)	$150,735
Noncash Expenses		
Depreciation	$2,045	$4,090
Amortization	253	506
Subtotal	$2,298	$4,596
Total Expenses	$484,111	$741,472
Increase in Unrestricted Net Assets		
(Profit)	($58,369)	$146,139

CHAPTER 6

Natural and Functional Statements of Activity

IN EARLIER CHAPTERS, the Statement of Activity was discussed and modified to enable management to better understand the statement and be in a position to take corrective action. The Statement of Activity was also discussed in the context of providing budget information.

The Natural Basis

The Statements of Activity illustrated in Exhibits 1.2, 3.1, and 5.1 were based on the natural method of presenting revenues and expenses. Statements based on this method classify revenues and expenses according to their natural category: dues were shown as total dues, salaries as total salaries, and so forth. Natural Statements of Activity do not assign revenues and expenses to specific activities or departments of the organization.

The consolidated Statement of Activity, though important, does not provide management with the information it needs to ensure fiscal accountability or serve as the basis of a good budgeting system.

The Functional Basis

Management requires more detail than the consolidated Statement of Activity provides. The statement needs to be expanded by assigning revenues and expenses to the specific departments responsible for earning revenues and incurring expenses. When revenues and expenses are assigned to specific activities, the resulting statement is said to be prepared on the functional basis.

Functions of a not-for-profit organization may include administration, membership, editorial, and conferences, among others. When prepared on the functional basis, the Statement of Activity illustrated in Exhibit 5.1 may appear as shown in Exhibit 6.1.

The Functional Statement of Activity provides management with information on how individual departments of the organization are performing. Decisions will now be based on individual department performance. Note that financial statements audited by independent CPA firms must be presented in the audited financial statements in the functional format.

EXHIBIT 6.1

Sample Functional Statement of Activity

Functional Statement of Activity
(Functional Income Statement)
February 28, 20X0

	Administration	Membership	Editorial	Conferences
Revenues				
Dues		$576,398		
Publication Sales			$107,834	
Less Cost of Goods Sold			(38,950)	
Advertising			77,250	
Interest	$4,359			
Conferences				
Registrations				$130,780
Exhibits				22,700
Other	7,240			
Total Revenues	$11,599	$576,398	$146,134	$153,480
Expenses				
Controllable Expenses				
Salaries	$83,405	$102,766	$152,532	$67,057
Travel	12,680	9,050		3,741
Printing	3,902	10,405	48,457	
Postage	4,005	10,093	2,232	1,768
Supplies	535	871	305	342
Telephone	452	4,500	4,761	2,392
Independent Contractors	16,690			
Miscellaneous	974	1,002	537	690
Subtotal	$122,643	$138,687	$208,823	$75,990
Semi-Controllable Expenses				
Fringe Benefits	$9,387	$11,584	$17,217	$7,602
Payroll Taxes	6,845	8,448	11,887	6,211
Other Taxes	7,368	2,042	1,090	542
Utilities	994	1,227	1,822	805
Insurance	2,050			
Subtotal	$26,644	$23,301	$32,016	$15,160
Fixed Expenses				
Rent	$12,300	$15,180	$22,560	$9,960
Interest	26,800			
Lease Contracts		1,140	2,964	
Maintenance Contracts	2,608			
Depreciation	4,090			
Amortization	506			
Subtotal	$46,304	$16,320	$25,524	$9,960
Total Expenses	$178,901	$178,408	$283,053	$101,110
Increase (Decrease) in Unrestricted Net Assets	($167,302)	$397,990	($136,919)	$52,370

CHAPTER 7

Internal Financial Statements

THE FINANCIAL STATEMENTS illustrated in the preceding chapters were developed to demonstrate how financial statements may be constructed and to serve as a guide to customizing financial statements that will meet the needs of the organization while also serving as a budgeting tool. These statements will now be amended further to include budget as well as actual figures.

Budgeting philosophies, procedures, and forms are discussed at length in later chapters. An organization implementing or changing its budgeting system should, however, be satisfied with the basic financial statements before budgeting policy is implemented.

Internal financial statements should be developed to meet the needs of the organization and to serve as the basis for business decisions. Except for the Statement of Financial Position (balance sheet), internal financial statements should include actual and budget figures for both current month and year to date along with the resulting variance. These internal financial statements also should include the total annual budget figures by line item on the monthly financial statements and the actual figures for the prior year by line item as a reference point.

Internal financial statements should be prepared monthly and, at a minimum, should include the following:

➢ Statement of Financial Position

➢ Consolidated Statement of Activity (Exhibit 7.1)

➢ Statements of Activity by function (Exhibits 7.2 through 7.5)

EXHIBIT 7.1

Sample Consolidated Statement of Activity

Consolidated Statement of Activity
For the Two-Month Period Ended February 28, 20X0

Current Month					Year to Date				
Prior Year Actual	Current Year Budget	Current Year Actual	Variance		Prior Year Actual	Current Year Budget	Current Year Actual	Variance	Total Current Year Budget
				Revenues					
$268,308	$275,000	$278,050	$3,050	Dues	$540,626	$575,134	$576,398	$1,264	$3,358,388
48,700	50,000	51,360	1,360	Publication Sales	102,177	106,000	107,834	1,834	657,004
(14,610)	(15,000)	(15,780)	(780)	Less Cost of Goods Sold	(33,758)	(37,000)	(38,950)	(1,950)	(243,700)
36,000	38,000	36,480	(1,520)	Advertising	78,500	80,000	77,250	(2,750)	465,500
1,950	2,000	2,141	141	Interest	4,111	4,200	4,359	159	30,154
				Conference					
54,974	56,000	58,888	2,888	Registrations	124,422	126,000	130,780	4,780	250,000
11,000	11,000	10,700	(300)	Exhibits	23,200	23,200	22,700	(500)	30,000
				All Other					
3,297	3,500	3,903	403	Revenues	6,833	7,000	7,240	240	50,000
$409,619	$420,500	$425,742	$5,242	**Total Revenues**	$846,111	$884,534	$887,611	$3,077	$4,597,346
				Expenses					
				Controllable Expenses					
$265,050	$275,000	$283,290	$1,710	Salaries	$379,986	$404,240	$405,760	($1,520)	$2,534,560
5,037	6,000	5,043	957	Travel	25,474	27,403	25,471	1,932	150,826
43,902	45,000	46,644	(1,644)	Printing	56,655	61,500	62,764	(1,264)	366,584
7,506	8,000	8,309	(309)	Postage	16,670	18,000	18,098	(98)	110,000
1,107	12,000	1,002	198	Supplies	1,843	2,000	2,052	(52)	12,300
1,305	1,400	1,303	97	Telephone	10,977	12,000	12,205	(205)	75,000
7,200	8,000	8,340	(340)	Independent Contractors	13,703	15,000	16,690	(1,690)	100,000
				Miscellaneous					
1,353	1,500	1,566	(66)	Expenses	2,989	3,150	3,203	(53)	19,250
$332,460	$356,100	$355,497	$603	Subtotal	$508,297	$543,293	$546,243	($2,950)	$3,368,520

EXHIBIT 7.1 *(Continued)*

Prior Year Actual	Current Year Budget	Current Year Actual	Variance		Prior Year Actual	Current Year Budget	Current Year Actual	Variance	Total Current Year Budget
Current Month					**Year to Date**				
				Semi-Controllable Expenses					
$37,207	$40,000	$39,404	$596	Fringe Benefits	$43,337	$46,104	$45,790	$314	$275,740
23,948	25,750	26,426	(676)	Payroll Taxes	30,785	32,750	33,391	(641)	199,346
9,200	9,500	10,000	(500)	Other Taxes	9,680	10,750	11,042	(292)	67,252
2,454	2,650	2,705	(55)	Utilities	4,212	4,750	4,848	(98)	30,000
950	1,025	1,025	0	Insurance	1,909	2,050	2,050	0	12,300
$73,759	$78,925	$79,560	($635)	Subtotal	$89,923	$96,404	$97,121	($717)	$584,638
				Fixed Expenses					
$28,200	$30,000	$30,000	$0	Rent	$56,400	$60,000	$60,000	$0	$360,000
14,100	13,400	13,400	0	Interest	28,200	26,800	26,800	0	160,800
1,980	2,052	2,052	0	Lease Contracts	3,960	4,104	4,104	0	24,624
1,133	1,304	1,304	0	Maintenance Contracts	2,266	2,608	2,608	0	15,648
1,890	2,045	2,045	0	Depreciation	3,780	4,090	4,090	0	24,540
409	253	253	0	Amortization	818	506	506	0	3,036
$47,712	$49,054	$49,054	$0	Subtotal	$95,424	$98,108	$98,108	$0	$588,648
$453,931	$484,079	$484,111	($32)	Total Expenses	$693,644	$737,805	$741,472	($3,667)	$4,541,806
($44,312)	($63,579)	($58,369)	$5,210	Increase (Decrease) in Unrestricted Net Assets	$152,467	$146,729	$146,139	$590	$55,540

EXHIBIT 7.2

Sample Statement of Activity for Administration Department

Statement of Activity–Administration Department
For the Two-Month Period Ended February 28, 20X0

Current Month					Year to Date				Total
Prior Year Actual	Current Year Budget	Current Year Actual	Variance		Prior Year Actual	Current Year Budget	Current Year Actual	Variance	Current Year Budget
				Revenues					
$1,950	$2,000	$2,141	$141	Interest	$4,111	$4,200	$4,359	$159	$30,154
				All Other					
3,297	3,500	3,903	403	Revenues	6,800	7,000	7,240	240	50,000
$5,247	$5,500	$6,044	$544	Total Revenues	$10,944	$11,200	$11,599	$399	$80,154
				Expenses					
				Controllable Expenses					
$58,280	$62,000	$61,702	$298	Salaries	$78,020	$83,000	$83,405	($405)	$519,584
2,705	3,000	2,703	297	Travel	12,797	13,000	12,680	320	74,960
1,977	2,000	1,951	49	Printing	3,823	4,000	3,902	98	23,400
1,725	1,780	1,828	(48)	Postage	3,794	3,900	4,005	(105)	23,870
268	275	261	14	Supplies	527	550	535	15	3,198
45	50	48	2	Telephone	455	475	452	23	2,775
				Miscellaneous					
444	450	476	(26)	Expenses	851	875	974	(99)	5,775
$65,444	$69,555	$68,969	$586	Subtotal	$100,267	$105,800	$105,953	($153)	$653,562
				Semi-Controllable Expenses					
$7,316	$8,400	$8,039	$361	Fringe Benefits	$8,883	$9,451	$9,387	$64	$56,527
4,607	5,175	5,390	(215)	Payroll Taxes	6,280	6,680	6,845	(165)	40,668
6,236	6,290	6,670	(380)	Other Taxes	6,246	7,170	7,368	(198)	44,858
450	530	556	(26)	Utilities	525	876	994	(118)	6,150
950	1,025	1,025	0	Insurance	1,909	2,050	2,050	0	12,300
$19,559	$21,420	$21,680	($260)	Subtotal	$23,843	$26,227	$26,644	($417)	$160,503
				Fixed Expenses					
$8,225	$8,750	$8,750	$0	Rent	$11,563	$12,300	$12,300	$0	$73,800
14,100	13,400	13,400	0	Interest	28,200	26,800	26,800	0	160,800
1,133	1,304	1,304	0	Maintenance	2,266	2,608	2,608	0	15,648
				Contracts					
1,890	2,045	2,045	0	Depreciation	3,780	4,090	4,090	0	24,540
409	253	253	0	Amortization	818	506	506	0	3,036
$25,757	$25,752	$25,752	$0	Subtotal	$46,627	$46,304	$46,304	$0	$277,824
$110,760	$116,727	$116,401	$326	Total Expenses	$170,737	$178,331	$178,901	($570)	$1,091,889
				Increase (Decrease) in Unrestricted					
($105,513)	($111,227)	($110,357)	$870	Net Assets	($159,793)	($16,131)	($167,302)	($171)	($1,011,735)

EXHIBIT 7.3

Sample Statement of Activity for Membership Department

Statement of Activity–Membership Department
For the Two-Month Period Ended February 28, 20X0

Current Month					Year to Date				
Prior Year Actual	Current Year Budget	Current Year Actual	Variance		Prior Year Actual	Current Year Budget	Current Year Actual	Variance	Total Current Year Budget
				Revenues					
$268,308	$275,000	$278,050	$3,050	Dues	$540,626	$575,134	$576,398	$1,264	$3,358,388
				Expenses					
				Controllable Expenses					
$67,680	$72,000	$71,383	$617	Salaries	$95,880	$102,000	$102,766	($766)	$641,243
920	1,000	1,003	(3)	Travel	9,049	9,500	9,050	450	53,543
5,344	5,500	5,308	192	Printing	9,944	10,600	10,405	195	62,400
3,906	4,100	4,156	(56)	Postage	9,568	10,000	10,093	(93)	61,600
427	450	421	29	Supplies	839	875	871	4	5,166
471	500	491	9	Telephone	4,098	4,250	4,600	(350)	28,200
483	500	485	15	Miscellaneous Expenses	902	975	1,002	(27)	5,968
$79,231	$84,050	$83,247	$803	Subtotal	$130,280	$138,200	$138,787	($587)	$858,120
				Semi-Controllable Expenses					
$9,292	$10,000	$9,969	$31	Fringe Benefits	$10,921	$11,618	$11,584	$34	$69,486
6,110	6,500	6,686	(186)	Payroll Taxes	7,789	8,286	8,448	(162)	50,434
1,599	1,760	1,850	(90)	Other Taxes	1,898	1,989	2,042	(53)	12,441
607	675	684	(9)	Utilities	1,206	1,300	1,227	73	7,590
$17,608	$18,935	$19,189	($254)	Subtotal	$21,814	$23,193	$23,301	($108)	$139,951
				Fixed Expenses					
$4,700	$5,000	$5,000	$0	Rent	$14,269	$15,180	$15,180	$0	$91,080
550	570	570	0	Lease Contract	1,101	1,140	1,140	0	6,845
$5,250	$5,570	$5,570	$0	Subtotal	$15,370	$16,320	$16,320	$0	$97,925
$102,089	$108,555	$108,006	$549	**Total Expenses**	$167,464	$177,713	$178,408	($695)	$1,095,996
				Increase (Decrease) in Unrestricted					
$166,219	$166,445	$170,044	$3,599	**Net Assets**	$373,162	$397,421	$397,990	$569	$2,262,392

EXHIBIT 7.4

Sample Statement of Activity for Editorial Department

Statement of Activity—Editorial Department
For the Two-Month Period Ended February 28, 20X0

Current Month					Year to Date				
Prior Year Actual	Current Year Budget	Current Year Actual	Variance		Prior Year Actual	Current Year Budget	Current Year Actual	Variance	Total Current Year Budget
				Revenues					
$48,700	$50,000	$51,360	$1,360	Publication Sales	$102,177	$106,000	$107,834	$1,834	$657,004
(14,610)	(15,000)	(15,780)	(780)	Less Cost of Goods Sold	(33,758)	(37,000)	(38,950)	(1,950)	(243,700)
36,000	38,000	36,480	(1,520)	Advertising	78,500	80,000	77,250	(2,750)	465,500
$70,090	$73,000	$72,060	($940)	Total Revenues	$146,919	$149,000	$146,134	($2,866)	$878,804
				Expenses					
				Controllable Expenses					
$91,180	$97,000	$96,266	$734	Salaries	$142,880	$152,000	$152,532	($532)	$952,995
36,581	37,500	39,385	(1,885)	Printing	42,888	46,900	48,457	(1,557)	280,784
925	1,000	987	13	Postage	1,900	2,100	2,232	(132)	13,200
142	160	150	10	Supplies	260	275	304	(29)	1,500
508	550	508	42	Telephone	4,404	4,600	4,761	(161)	29,250
7,200	8,000	8,340	(340)	Independent Contractors	13,703	15,000	16,690	(1,690)	100,000
276	300	261	39	Miscellaneous Expenses	573	600	537	63	3,215
$136,812	$144,510	$145,897	($1,387)	Subtotal	$206,608	$221,475	$225,513	($4,038)	$1,380,944
				Semi-Controllable Expenses					
$14,107	$15,000	$14,816	$184	Fringe Benefits	$16,252	$17,289	$17,017	$72	$103,678
8,719	9,275	9,408	(133)	Payroll Taxes	11,959	11,659	11,887	(228)	70,967
905	975	990	(15)	Other Taxes	1,031	1,064	1,090	(26)	6,658
990	1,000	1,014	(14)	Utilities	1,705	1,781	1,822	(41)	11,250
$24,721	$26,250	$26,228	$22	Subtotal	$29,947	$31,793	$31,816	($223)	$192,553
				Fixed Expenses					
$10,575	$11,250	$11,250	$0	Rent	$21,206	$22,560	$22,560	$0	$135,000
1,430	1,482	1,482	0	Lease Contracts	2,859	2,964	2,964	0	17,779
$12,005	$12,732	$12,732	$0	Subtotal	$24,065	$25,524	$25,524	$0	$152,779
$173,538	$183,492	$184,857	($1,365)	**Total Expenses**	$260,620	$278,792	$283,053	($4,261)	$1,726,267
				Increase (Decrease) in Unrestricted Net Assets					
($103,448)	($110,492)	($112,797)	($2,305)		($113,701)	($129,792)	($136,919)	($7,127)	($847,472)

EXHIBIT 7.5

Sample Statement of Activity for Conference Department

Statement of Activity—Conference Department
For the Two-Month Period Ended February 28, 20X0

Current Month					Year to Date				
Prior Year Actual	Current Year Budget	Current Year Actual	Variance		Prior Year Actual	Current Year Budget	Current Year Actual	Variance	Total Current Year Budget
				Revenues					
				Conference					
$54,974	$56,000	$58,888	$2,888	Registrations	$124,422	$126,000	$130,780	$4,780	$250,000
11,000	11,000	10,700	(300)	Exhibits	23,200	23,200	22,700	(500)	30,000
$65,974	$67,000	$69,588	$2,588	Total Revenues	$147,622	$149,200	$153,480	$4,280	$280,000
				Expenses					
				Controllable Expenses					
$47,910	$54,000	$53,939	$61	Salaries	$63,206	$67,240	$67,057	$183	$420,738
1,412	2,000	1,337	663	Travel	3,628	4,903	3,741	1,162	22,323
950	1,120	1,338	(218)	Postage	1,408	2,000	1,768	232	11,330
270	315	170	145	Supplies	217	300	342	(42)	2,436
281	300	256	44	Telephone	2,020	2,675	2,392	283	14,775
150	250	344	(94)	Miscellaneous Expenses	663	700	690	10	4,292
$50,973	$57,985	$57,384	$601	Subtotal	$71,142	$77,818	$75,990	$1,828	$475,894
				Semi-Controllable Expenses					
$6,492	$6,600	$6,580	$20	Fringe Benefits	$7,281	$7,746	$7,602	$144	$46,049
4,512	4,800	4,942	(142)	Payroll Taxes	5,757	6,125	6,211	(86)	37,277
460	475	490	(15)	Other Taxes	505	527	542	(15)	3,295
407	445	451	(6)	Utilities	776	793	805	(12)	5,010
$11,871	$12,320	$12,463	($143)	Subtotal	$14,319	$15,191	$15,160	$31	$91,631
				Fixed Expenses					
$4,700	$5,000	$5,000	$0	Rent	$9,362	$9,960	$9,960	$0	$60,120
$67,544	$75,305	$74,847	$458	Total Expenses	$94,823	$102,969	$101,110	$1,859	$627,645
				Increase (Decrease) in Unrestricted					
($1,570)	($8,305)	($5,259)	$3,046	Net Assets	$52,799	$46,231	$52,370	$6,139	($347,645)

CHAPTER 8

Budgeting Philosophy

WHAT IS A BUDGET? Informally, it is an educated guess. Formally, it is a process of establishing a financial goal for the future and of monitoring the progress toward that goal by comparing the goal with actual results.

Budgets have two separate sets of goals:

➤ Statement of Activity (income statement) goals

➤ Statement of Financial Position (balance sheet) goals

In commercial organizations, the budget ensures that revenues exceed expenses, resulting in a profit. In not-for-profit organizations, the budget ensures that revenues are available to continue programs and services for the membership.

The Long-Range Plan and Short-Term Budget

The long-range plan usually covers a span of five or more years. The short-term budget is usually for one or two years.

Budgeting Tools

The following tools are necessary for effective budgeting:

➤ Accurate historical data—at least five years of data, for evaluating trends

➤ Easy-to-understand forms and processes

Eight Steps for an Effective Budget

1. Know your organization's mission.
   Write down your organization's mission on the back of your business card. Which statement better describes your budget decisions?

> ➤ They are moving you closer to achieving your mission.
> ➤ They are moving you away from accomplishing your mission.

2. Make sure that everyone involved in the budget process understands elementary accounting principles.

3. Design the budget process to be simple, consistent, and easy to understand.

4. Make sure that all those involved in the budget process know their roles.

5. Tie the budget into the organization's long-range plan.

6. Make sure the organization has an effective budget approval process.

7. Once the process is implemented, track its progress toward the budgeted goals by analyzing monthly financial statements.

8. If budgeting problems exist, be prepared to correct them through formal plans of action to offset negative budget variances.

CHAPTER 9

Continuous Budgeting System Overview

AN OVERVIEW OF THIS new budgeting system is necessary if management intends to implement the policies and forms discussed and shown in this handbook. Many policies and forms are interdependent and must be implemented and used together to achieve the desired results.

This system begins with the distribution of monthly financial statements (Exhibit 9.1). These monthly statements should be prepared and distributed to the chief executive officer (CEO) and managers within 10 working days after the close of the prior month. Proper timing of these monthly financial statements is essential if management wants to be in a proactive rather than a reactive position to correct budgetary problems. The sooner management recognizes that problems exist, the faster corrective plans of action can be implemented. If too much time elapses between the end of the month and the distribution of the financial statements, valuable time that could have been used to correct problems will have been lost.

Once managers receive the monthly financial statements, they have two responsibilities:

➢ They must analyze and detail the revenue and controllable expenses credited and charged to their departments in the current month while that information is fresh in their minds and readily available.

➢ They must report on what went right and what went wrong for the prior month and what they could have done differently if they had been able. Once these tasks have been completed, managers will budget for the same revenue and expense items that they have just analyzed for the same month of the next year.

This continuous, or rolling, approach to budgeting has two advantages over other budgeting systems:

➤ It breaks down time-consuming annual budgeting processes into 12 easily manageable budget increments.

➤ It results in an accurate and detailed budget.

It is important for the CEO to hold a monthly budget meeting. At this meeting, managers report on the actual-versus-budget detail for the prior month and submit the preliminary budgets for the same month next year for consideration by higher management.

The CEO reviews and adjusts the preliminary monthly budgets submitted by management. Managers then submit these budgets to the budget coordinator, who updates the master budget. When it's time to prepare for the annual budget, the work is virtually complete because it has been done in 12 manageable monthly increments. Only fine-tuning will be necessary to complete the annual budget documents.

The key to the success of this system is the competence of the budget coordinator. This person typically will be responsible for the technical aspects of the budget, such as accurate depreciation calculations, cash flow projections, inventory valuations, and any other budget responsibility that has not been assigned to other managers.

This system is easy to implement, is easy to manage, requires much less staff time, ensures true fiscal accountability, predicts cash flow, and results in a far more accurate budget than traditional budgeting approaches.

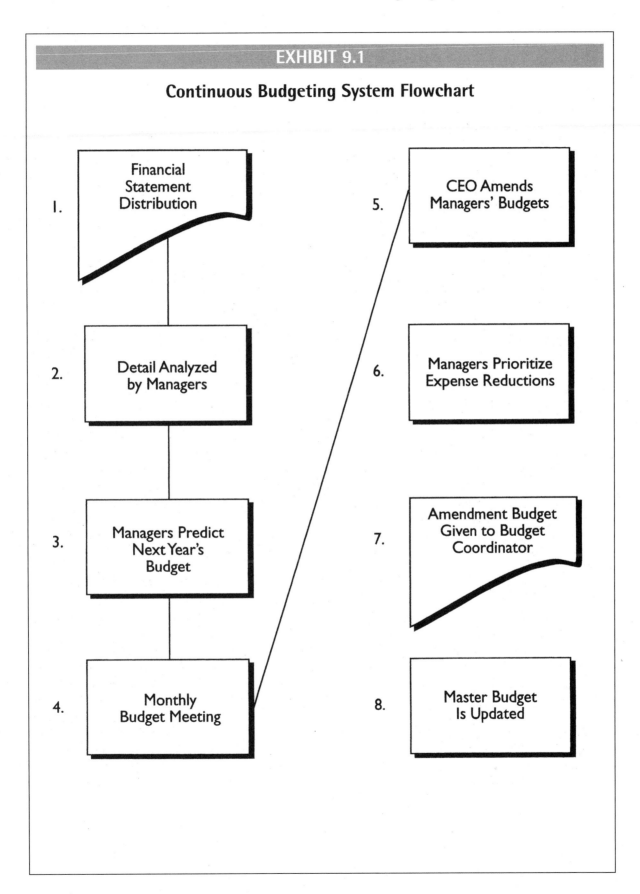

EXHIBIT 9.1

Continuous Budgeting System Flowchart

1. Financial Statement Distribution

2. Detail Analyzed by Managers

3. Managers Predict Next Year's Budget

4. Monthly Budget Meeting

5. CEO Amends Managers' Budgets

6. Managers Prioritize Expense Reductions

7. Amendment Budget Given to Budget Coordinator

8. Master Budget Is Updated

CHAPTER 10

The Executive and the Budget Process

MORE NOT–FOR–PROFIT organization executives lose their jobs because of poor financial management skills than for any other reason. It is typical for a not-for-profit organization to have a board of directors, a chairman of the board, a president, a treasurer, an executive committee, and a budget and finance committee. Unfortunately, the staff executive is usually held primarily responsible and accountable for fiscal problems. This reality is further complicated by the fact that few executives of not-for-profit organizations have formal accounting and financial management backgrounds. Not-for-profit organization executives who lack formal financial skills but have budgetary responsibility should educate themselves in this area by taking elementary college accounting classes and by attending educational seminars.

Accounting is the basis for business decisions. Those without formal financial training cannot make prudent business decisions based on financial statements because they do not really understand the statements. In addition, executives who have not been motivated to improve their understanding of accounting and finance will find they must rely on the organization's accounting staff. In this situation, the executive's career is in the hands of the organization's accountants. Management must take the necessary steps to ensure that the accounting staff is competent in Generally Accepted Accounting Principles (GAAP) for not-for-profit organizations.

Executives with budgeting responsibilities can greatly enhance career advancement and job security and also stabilize the general financial operation of the organization if they follow four simple rules:

➤ Ensure that the accounting function is staffed by competent people.

➤ Insist on timely, understandable financial statements that meet the organization's needs.

➤ Have a formal manual on accounting policies and procedures that is approved by the board of directors.

➤ Develop and administer a budget that is realistic and ensures true fiscal accountability.

Potential Budgeting Problems

The following are a few potential problems organizations may have with their budgeting systems:

An Obsolete Budgeting Process—It is typical for an organization's budgeting process to be an expensive, time-consuming, and dreaded task that results in endless hours of wasted time that should be spent on more productive activities. Despite good-faith efforts to produce an effective budget, the budget often is a carbon copy of the previous year's actual activity, adjusted for inflation and divided into 12 monthly increments.

Lack of Ongoing Fiscal Accountability—Often not-for-profit organization managers are not involved in the budget preparation process and are not held accountable for explaining and correcting budget deficiencies. The resulting lack of efficient fiscal accountability could cause problems over time.

Lack of Formal Plans of Action to Offset Negative Budget Variances—Not-for-profit organizations that lack formal plans of action to offset negative budget variances will inevitably make decisions that will be hasty rather than well thought out. Hasty decisions can result in unexpected consequences for which the association executive will ultimately be held responsible.

Poor Budget Approval Process—The budget approval process for not-for-profit organizations is unique because authority to approve the budget is the responsibility of volunteer members who are not involved with the management of the organization on a daily basis. If budget approval documents are cumbersome, hard to understand, and lacking in detail and explanation, a smooth budget approval process is unlikely.

Incomplete and Inadequate Budgets—Most budgets for not-for-profit organizations are woefully inadequate in that the budget is merely a projection of revenues and expenses called the operating budget. This is only one part of a budget that should have four components. A well-prepared budget should include a cash flow budget, a capital purchases budget, an inventory acquisition budget, and the operating budget. All four budgets are necessary to effectively plan the financial affairs of the organization (See Exhibit 10.1).

An executive burdened with an obsolete budgeting process that does not enforce fiscal accountability is being controlled by the organization rather than controlling it.

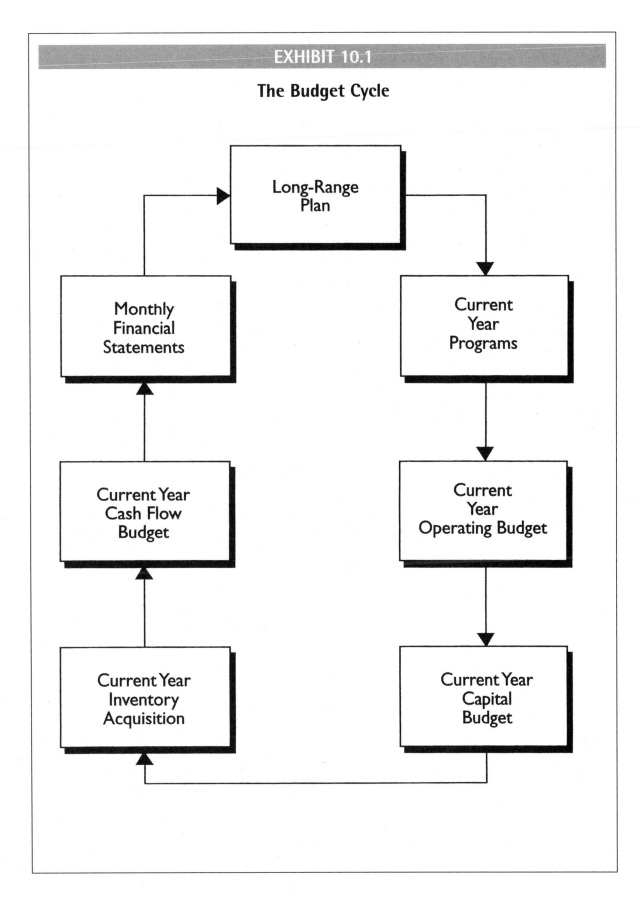

EXHIBIT 10.1

The Budget Cycle

These problems are solvable and can be corrected by an executive who is serious about setting up the necessary processes and forms required to get the job done.

The budgeting and ongoing financial management systems described in detail in later chapters are easy to implement and require little management time. The systems will result in an accurate and detailed budget. The chief executive officer should insist on implementation of a new and better budgeting system and will manage more effectively when the benefits of a good budget are realized.

Should an executive who is not the chief executive officer and who does not have authority to make sweeping organization-wide changes consider using the budgeting systems described in this book? Absolutely. This budgeting system can be applied to components of the organization's activities. The management of the affected department will improve markedly over that of departments using less effective methods.

A good budget is an effective management tool when prepared and administered properly. Managers must take the time to digest the forms and systems described in this handbook and customize them for use in their organizations or departments. A manager's effectiveness, and career advancement potential, will benefit from a proactive approach to implementing a better budgeting and financial management system.

Expense Reduction Plans

FINANCIAL AND BUDGET problems are inevitable, even in the most stable organizations. Despite this inevitability, few organizations have formal plans about what action they will take when faced with financial problems. If an organization has no formal plan of action to offset negative budget variances, management will implement hasty decisions that may cause problems.

The easiest way to implement a plan of action to offset negative budget variances is to have managers complete an expense reduction plan in conjunction with their monthly budget responsibilities. Unfavorable budget variances should be addressed by a plan that will reduce expenses rather than rely on an unpredictable increase in revenues. Expense reduction plans should be based on realistic percentages and should be applied to the controllable and semi-controllable expenses charged to each department. An example of how to communicate this to the Membership Department manager is shown in Exhibit 11.1.

It is also advisable to regularly communicate to the entire staff the financial health of the organization and what action will be taken if cost-cutting measures are necessary. This communication alleviates fear, improves morale, and gives staff the impression that the organization is being run professionally and managed prudently. A sample memorandum is shown in Exhibit 11.2.

EXHIBIT 11.1

Sample Form for Expense Reduction Plan

Membership Department
Expense Reduction Plan
Affected Month—February 28, 20X1

The budget for your department is based on the assumption that revenues and expenses are realistic and attainable. Indicate your plan for a 5 percent reduction in the controllable and semi-controllable expenses charged to the Membership Department in the event that economic conditions force expense reductions.

_____

_____

_____

_____

_____

_____

_____

_____

_____

_____

_____

_____

_____

_____

_____

_____

EXHIBIT 11.2

Sample Memorandum on Cost-Cutting Measures

Date: March 15, 20X0

To: All Staff

From: Executive Director

Re: Plan of Action to Offset Negative Budget Variances

While we feel the organization's operating budget is realistic and attainable, prudent fiscal management must allow for the fact that economic factors beyond our control may have an adverse financial effect on the organization.

If this situation should occur, employees should be aware that expense reductions have been analyzed and priorities set by each department. Reducing staff will be a last resort.

If adverse financial conditions do force us to implement expense reductions, you can expect these reductions to be carried out quickly.

CHAPTER 12

The Monthly Budget Process

THE **BUDGETING PROCESS** described in this manual is called continuous budgeting. The monthly budgeting process begins with the distribution of a packet of information, forms, and instructions to managers. Under ideal conditions, this information should be distributed within 10 working days after the close of the prior month. The packet of information typically would include the following:

- ➢ A memorandum of specific instructions, deadlines, meeting dates, and so forth (Exhibit 12.1)
- ➢ The department's Statement of Activity (Exhibit 12.2)
- ➢ An analysis of current-month data (Exhibit 12.3)
- ➢ A monthly report on activities (Exhibit 12.4)
- ➢ A subsequent-year budget projection (Exhibit 12.5)
- ➢ An inventory purchase request (Exhibit 12.6)
- ➢ A capital expenditure request (Exhibit 12.7)
- ➢ An expense reduction plan (Exhibit 12.8)

EXHIBIT 12.1

Sample Memorandum of Instructions

To: Membership Manager

From: Chief Executive Officer

Date: March 10, 20X0

Re: Financial Statements/Continuous Budget

Attached are the Membership Department's financial statements for the two-month period ending February 28, 20X0. Be advised that the monthly budget meeting is scheduled for March 15, 20X0, at 10:00 A.M. You should be prepared to bring the following:

➢ A completed analysis of current-month data
➢ A completed monthly report on activities
➢ A completed subsequent-year budget projection
➢ A completed inventory purchase request
➢ A completed capital expenditure request
➢ A completed expense reduction plan

EXHIBIT 12.2

Sample Statement of Activity for Membership Department

Statement of Activity—Membership Department
For the Two-Month Period Ended February 28, 20X0

| Current Month | | | | | Year to Date | | | | Total |
Prior Year Actual	Current Year Budget	Current Year Actual	Variance		Prior Year Actual	Current Year Budget	Current Year Actual	Variance	Current Year Budget
				Revenues					
$268,308	$275,000	$278,050	$3,050	Dues	$540,626	$575,134	$576,398	$1,264	$3,358,388
				Expenses					
				Controllable Expenses					
$67,680	$72,000	$71,383	$617	Salaries	$95,880	$102,000	$102,766	($766)	$641,243
920	1,000	1,003	(3)	Travel	9,049	9,500	9,050	450	53,543
5,344	5,500	5,308	192	Printing	9,944	10,600	10,405	195	62,400
3,906	4,100	4,156	(56)	Postage	9,568	10,000	10,093	(93)	61,600
427	450	421	29	Supplies	839	875	871	4	5,166
471	500	491	9	Telephone	4,098	4,250	4,600	(350)	28,200
483	500	485	15	Miscellaneous Expenses	902	975	1,002	(27)	5,968
$79,231	$84,050	$83,247	$803	Subtotal	$130,280	$138,200	$138,787	($587)	$858,120
				Semi-Controllable Expenses					
$9,292	$10,000	$9,969	$31	Fringe Benefits	$10,921	$11,618	$11,584	$34	$69,486
6,110	6,500	6,686	(186)	Payroll Taxes	7,789	8,286	8,448	(162)	50,434
1,599	1,760	1,850	(90)	Other Taxes	1,898	1,989	2,042	(53)	12,441
607	675	684	(9)	Utilities	1,206	1,300	1,227	73	7,590
$17,608	$18,935	$19,189	($254)	Subtotal	$21,814	$23,193	$23,301	($108)	$139,951
				Fixed Expenses					
$4,700	$5,000	$5,000	$0	Rent	$14,269	$15,180	$15,180	$0	$91,080
550	570	570	0	Lease Contracts	1,101	1,140	1,140	0	6,845
$5,250	$5,570	$5,570	$0	Subtotal	$15,370	$16,320	$16,320	$0	$97,925
$102,089	$108,555	$108,006	$549	**Total Expenses**	$167,464	$177,713	$178,408	($695)	$1,095,996
				Increase (Decrease) in Unrestricted					
$166,219	$166,445	$170,044	$3,599	**Net Assets**	$373,162	$397,421	$397,990	$569	$2,262,392

EXHIBIT 12.3

Sample Form for Analysis of Current-Month Data

Analysis of Current-Month Data
Membership Department
February 28, 20X0

After each item, provide a detailed analysis of actual figures for the current month and an explanation of variances.

	Budget	Actual	Variance
Revenues: Dues	$275,000	$278,050	$3,050

_____

_____

	Budget	Actual	Variance
Controllable Expenses:			
Salaries	$72,000	$71,383	$617

			Leave Hours		
Employee Name	Regular Wages	Overtime Wages	Annual	Sick	Personal
___	___	___	___	___	___
___	___	___	___	___	___
___	___	___	___	___	___
___	___	___	___	___	___

	Budget	Actual	Variance
Travel	$1,000	$1,003	($3)

_____

_____

_____

	EXHIBIT 12.3 *(Continued)*		
Printing	**Budget** $5,500	Actual $5,308	Variance $192

	Budget	Actual	Variance
Postage	**Budget** $4,100	Actual $4,156	Variance ($56)

	Budget	Actual	Variance
Supplies	**Budget** $450	Actual $421	Variance $29

	Budget	Actual	Variance
Telephone	**Budget** $500	Actual $491	Variance $9

	Budget	Actual	Variance
Miscellaneous	**Budget** $500	Actual $485	Variance $15

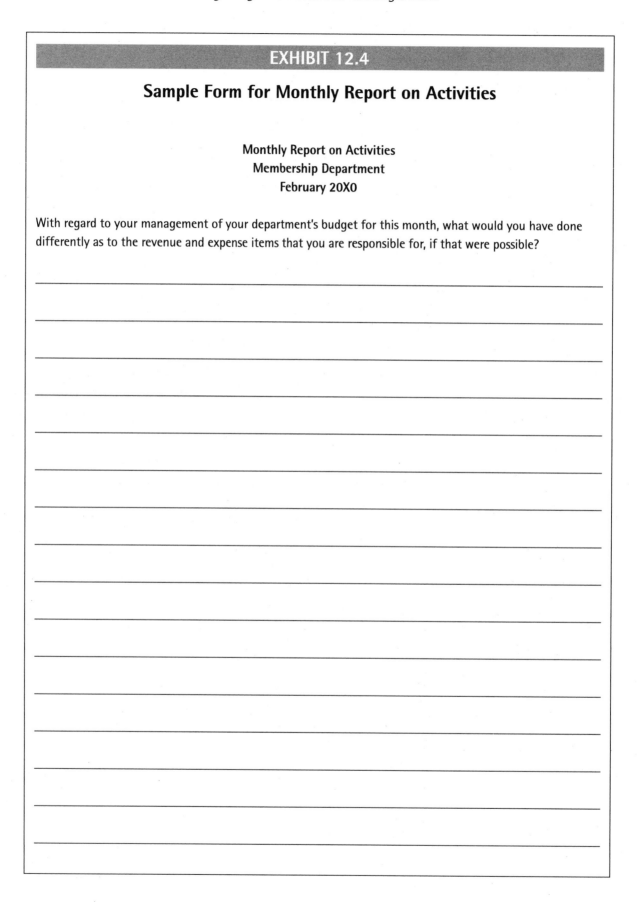

EXHIBIT 12.4

Sample Form for Monthly Report on Activities

Monthly Report on Activities
Membership Department
February 20X0

With regard to your management of your department's budget for this month, what would you have done differently as to the revenue and expense items that you are responsible for, if that were possible?

EXHIBIT 12.5

Sample Form for Subsequent-Year Budget Projection

Subsequent-Year Budget Projection
Membership Department
February 20X1

Based on your analysis of actual data for the month of February 20X0, detail and explain your predictions for the same revenues and expenses for February 20X1.

	Actual Feb. 20X0	Budget Feb. 20X1
Revenues: Dues	$278,050	$_____

_____

_____

_____

_____

Are there any revenue items not listed that will be credited to the Membership Department in February 20X1? Explain and budget accordingly.

	Budget Feb. 20X1
Item:_____	$_____

_____

_____

_____

_____

	Actual Feb. 20X0	Budget Feb. 20X1
Total Revenues	$278,050	$_____

EXHIBIT 12.5 *(Continued)*

Expenses

	Actual Feb. 20X0 $71,383		Budget Feb. 20X1 $_____	
Salaries				
Employee Name	**Regular Wages**	**Overtime Wages**	**Regular Wages**	**Overtime Wages**
_____	_____	_____	_____	_____
_____	_____	_____	_____	_____
_____	_____	_____	_____	_____
_____	_____	_____	_____	_____
Subtotals	$_____	$_____	$_____	$_____
Total Salaries	$_____		$_____	

	Actual Feb. 20X0	Budget Feb. 20X1
Travel	$1,003	$_____

	Actual Feb. 20X0	Budget Feb. 20X1
Printing	$5,308	$_____

	Actual Feb. 20X0	Budget Feb. 20X1
Postage	$4,156	$_____

_____

_____

_____

_____

	Actual Feb. 20X0	Budget Feb. 20X1
Supplies	$421	$_____

_____

_____

_____

_____

	Actual Feb. 20X0	Budget Feb. 20X1
Telephone	$491	$_____

_____

_____

_____

_____

	Actual Feb. 20X0	Budget Feb. 20X1
Miscellaneous	$485	$_____

_____

_____

_____

_____

EXHIBIT 12.5 (Continued)

EXHIBIT 12.5 *(Continued)*

Are there any expense items not listed that will be charged to the Membership Department in February 20X1? Explain and budget accordingly.

Budget
Feb. 20X1

Item:_____ $_____

_____

_____

_____

_____

Budget
Feb. 20X1

Item:_____ $_____

_____

_____

_____

_____

	Actual Feb. 20X0	Budget Feb. 20X1
Total Controllable Expenses	$83,247	$_____

Sample Form for Inventory Purchase Request

Inventory Purchase Request
Membership Department
February 20X1

Name of Item: _____

Intended Purchase Date: _____

Costs:

_____ $_____

_____   _____

_____   _____

_____   _____

Total Cash Required: $_____

Cost of Goods Sold Calculations

Total Cash Required		Quantity Purchased		Unit Cost of Goods Sold
$_____	÷		=	$_____

Gross Profit Per Unit

Selling Price per Unit		Unit Cost of Goods Sold		Gross Profit per Unit
$_____	−		=	$_____

Gross Profit Percentage

Gross Profit		Selling Price		Gross Profit %
$_____	÷	$	=	_____ %

EXHIBIT 12.7

Sample Form for Capital Expenditure Request

Capital Expenditure Request
Membership Department
February 20X1

Item(s) Requested:

_____

_____

Is equipment new_____ or replacement equipment_____?
If replacement equipment, describe old equipment:_____

_____

_____

_____

Intended purchase date: _____

Anticipated Costs:

Equipment Cost	$_____	Start-up Supplies	$_____
Installation Costs	$_____	Maintenance Contract	$_____
Sales Tax	$_____	Other Costs:	
Shipping Costs	$_____	_____	$_____
Insurance on Shipping	$_____	_____	$_____
Total	$_____	Total	$_____

Number of years equipment is expected to be used:_____.

FOR ACCOUNTING DEPARTMENT USE

EXHIBIT 12.8

Sample Form for Expense Reduction Plan

Expense Reduction Plan
Membership Department
Affected Month—February 20X1

The budget for your department is based on the assumption that revenues and expenses are realistic and attainable. Indicate your plan for a 5 percent reduction in the controllable and semi-controllable expenses charged to the Membership Department in the event that economic conditions force expense reductions.

_____

_____

_____

_____

_____

_____

_____

_____

_____

_____

_____

_____

_____

_____

_____

CHAPTER 13

The Cash Flow Budget

COMPILING AN EFFECTIVE cash flow budget is complicated because the receipt and disbursement of cash under the accrual basis of accounting usually are unrelated to the revenues, expenses, and results of operations. Sales usually are represented by additions to accounts receivable and not the receipt of cash. Some expenses do not involve disbursing cash (depreciation, for example), debt service does not appear at all, and so forth.

However complicated, cash flow budgets are necessary if an organization wants to maximize investment opportunities and ensure that enough cash is available to meet current obligations. An annual cash flow analysis should be prepared by the budget coordinator based on the monthly budget preparation.

Just as department managers are responsible for analyzing cash flow for the current month, the budget coordinator is responsible for analyzing current-month cash flow. The formula for a cash flow budget is simple:

Cash Balance, Beginning of Month	$
Plus Cash Received During Month	+ _____
Equals Cash Available for Month	=
Less Cash Disbursed During Month	− _____
Equals Cash Available, End of Month	= _____

This basic formula is then expanded to track cash flow through the various revenue, expense, and Statement of Financial Position accounts. Each account that involves the flow of cash is listed, and the accounts that do not involve the flow of cash are eliminated (Exhibit 13.1).

EXHIBIT 13.1

Monthly Cash Flow Analysis

Cash Balance, Beginning of Month		
+ Cash Received During Month:		$101,323
Dues	$25,048	
Collections on Accounts Receivable	10,900	
Cash Sales	5,766	
Office Sublease	5,000	
Deferred Conference Revenues	5,705	
Deferred Advertising Revenues	6,990	+ 59,409
− Cash Disbursed During Month:		
Salaries	$24,044	
Fringe Benefits	4,699	
Rent	15,000	
Debt Service	6,040	
Prepaid Expenses	2,398	
Insurance	1,204	
Supplies	2,193	
Purchase of Fixed Assets	5,700	
Purchase of Inventory	2,307	− 63,585
= Cash Available, End of Month		$91,147

Once the department budgets are prepared, the budget coordinator compiles them and projects the cash flow for the same month of the subsequent year. Once the current-month cash flow projections are completed, the totals are detailed in the consolidated cash flow budget (Exhibit 13.2). A properly prepared consolidated cash flow budget shows how much cash is available for investment and for how long.

Note that the end-of-month cash available becomes the beginning-of-month cash available for the next month. The determination of how much cash is available for investment and for how long is based on analysis of the end-of-month cash available for each month.

The actual investment decisions should be preapproved and detailed in the organization's accounting policy and procedures manual. The consolidated cash flow budget for the current year should be included with the budget documents submitted to the approving body.

EXHIBIT 13.2

Sample Consolidated Cash Flow Budget

Consolidated Cash Flow Budget
20X0

	Jan.	Feb.	Mar.	Apr.	May	Jun.	Jul.	Aug.	Sep.	Oct.	Nov.	Dec.
Cash Available, Beginning of Month	$101,323	$97,147	$117,992	$115,560	$102,679	$107,357	$98,720	$104,879	$106,725	$96,922	$115,914	$128,990
Plus Cash Received	59,409	69,940	73,123	47,120	93,010	81,981	72,205	73,911	51,513	69,069	68,088	70,047
Less Cash Disbursements	(63,585)	(49,095)	(75,555)	(60,001)	(88,332)	(90,618)	(66,046)	(72,065)	(61,316)	(50,077)	(55,012)	(62,709)
Equals Cash Available, End of Month	$97,147	$117,992	$115,560	$102,679	$107,357	$98,720	$104,879	$106,725	$96,922	$115,914	$128,990	$136,328

14

Getting the Budget Approved

THE FIRST STEP in establishing a smooth budget approval process is to communicate to managers what the current-year financial goals are before the annual budget process begins. The current-year financial goals should be related directly to the long-range plan's financial goals for the current year. Otherwise, a well-prepared budget could be presented to the approving body only to have it disapproved because the financial goals are unsatisfactory.

Determining Roles

The second step in the budget approval process is to decide on the roles and involvement of staff. Suggested roles for those involved in the budget process are described as follows.

Chief Executive Officer (CEO)

1. Tells staff how the budget relates to the long-range plan

2. Enforces deadlines and procedures

3. Reviews and negotiates with managers until objectives are met

Chief Financial Officer (CFO)/Budget Coordinator

1. Coordinates the budget process

2. Compiles data submitted by managers

3. Prepares the cash flow budget

4. Is responsible for budgeting for technical and uncontrollable expenses

5. Prepares the general administration budget at the direction of the CEO

6. Prepares final documents for the approving body

Staff Managers

1. Ensure that everyone in the department is involved in the budget process
2. Meet deadlines

Preparing and Presenting Financial Documents

The third step in the budget approval process is to prepare financial budget documents internally.

The fourth step is to forward the budget documents to the approving body before the budget approval meeting. These documents should meet the following criteria:

➤ They must be simple and easily understood.

➤ They must encourage questions before the meeting.

➤ They must detail trends.

➤ They must emphasize that the current-year budget meets the long-range plan's financial goals for the current year.

➤ They must explain the staff budgeting process.

The Approval Meeting

The fifth step in the budget approval process is to hold the budget approval meeting:

➤ The CEO should review the process.

➤ The CFO should be available to answer technical questions.

➤ The organization may consider having managers present their own budgets.

The sixth step in the budget approval process is approval.

Summary

1. Know the current financial year goal before starting, and ensure that the current-year budget relates to the long-range plan.

2. Decide on the roles and involvement of staff.

3. Prepare budget documents internally.

4. Forward budget documents to the approving body.

5. Host the budget approval meeting.

6. Obtain approval.

CHAPTER 15

Suggested Format of Budget Documents for an Approving Body

IF BUDGETING PROCESSES and forms described in this handbook have been used correctly, only fine-tuning will be required to complete the annual budget. The approving body should be provided with the information needed to approve the budget at the budget approval meeting. These documents should include the following:

➢ The operating budget

➢ Revenue trend analyses

➢ Expense trend analyses

➢ The capital budget

➢ The cash flow budget

➢ The inventory acquisition budget

Organizations should strive to prepare budget documents that will be forwarded to approving bodies in a format acceptable to the particular organization. The form of these documents is as important as the substance. If the documents look as if they have been professionally prepared, the approving body will view the budget as thorough and well thought out. A smooth approval process is likely if the documents meet these criteria:

1. They agree with the long-range plan's financial objective for the current year.

2. They are easy to read.

3. They are brief.

4. They avoid unnecessary detail.

5. Questions are anticipated and answered before they are asked.

Before the final documents are distributed, senior management should hold a rehearsal budget meeting. A few managers should assume the roles of members of the approving body and play devil's advocate by asking questions and critiquing the presentation. This exercise will make approval more likely.

An example of a budget package to be submitted to an approving body is shown in Exhibit 15.1.

Sample Budget Package for Submission to Approving Body

To: Executive Committee
From: Chief Executive Officer
Date: November 10, 20X0
Re: 20X1 Budget Proposal

Enclosed is the preliminary budget summary for our 20X1 fiscal year: January 1, 20X1, through December 31, 20X1. You should be aware of a few important points when reviewing the enclosed documents:

➢ We have budgeted for an increase in unrestricted net assets in the amount of $100,000. This figure meets our long-range plan's financial objectives.

➢ Also, in conjunction with the long-range plan, the documents reflect the new program of producing a monthly rather than a quarterly newsletter.

The budget approval meeting has been set for December 15, 20X0, at 10:00 A.M. We are optimistic that this meeting will be informative and satisfactory for the committee. For the meeting to go as smoothly as possible, I encourage you to contact our chief financial officer with any questions you may have regarding the budget. Please make this contact as far in advance of the meeting as possible.

Thank you. We look forward to a productive meeting.

EXHIBIT 15.1 *(Continued)*

Fiscal Year 20X1 Budget Proposal
Revenues

Item	Budget	Proposed Explanation
Dues	$3,699,172	Represents a projected net growth of 10%. Memberships are projected to increase from 24,468 on December 31, 20X0, to 26,915 on December 31, 20X1. No dues increase is reflected in this budget.
Publication Sales	755,557	Represents an increase of 15%. Five new books will be offered, and two will be discontinued.
Cost of Goods Sold	(241,778)	Cost of sales averages 32% for all publications combined.
Advertising	558,600	Increase of 20% projected from expanding the newsletter from quarterly to monthly.
Interest	27,139	Decrease of 1% projected from declining interest rates.
Conference Registrations	275,000	Projected advance registration delegates at $395 and on-site registration delegates at $455. No increase in the conference registration rates is reflected in this budget.
Conference Exhibits	35,000	Increase of $5,000 projected due to available exhibit hall space.
All Other Revenues	60,000	Several small revenue sources.
Total Budgeted Revenues	$5,168,690	

EXHIBIT 15.1 *(Continued)*

Five-Year Revenue Trends
and Fiscal Year 20X1 Revenue Budget

	Audited Actuals					Budget
Item	20Y1	20Y2	20Y3	20Y4	20X0	20X1
Dues	$2,231,022	$2,478,913	$2,785,296	$3,094,773	$3,363,884	$3,694,172
Publication Sales	440,018	489,243	562,444	631,852	679,411	755,557
Less Cost of Goods Sold	(132,005)	(146,773)	(168,733)	(189,556)	(203,823)	(241,778)
Advertising			286,830	375,309	460,933	558,600
Interest	19,412	22,922	25,408	27,809	29,414	27,139
Conferences						
Registrations	190,711	207,707	238,814	249,711	253,100	275,000
Exhibits	17,400	19,800	22,700	25,000	28,700	35,000
All Others	38,707	40,300	44,009	48,708	52,787	60,000
Total Revenues	$2,805,265	$3,112,112	$3,796,768	$4,263,606	$4,664,406	$5,163,690

EXHIBIT 15.1 *(Continued)*

Fiscal Year 20X1 Budget Proposal
Expenses

Item	Proposed Budget	Explanation
Controllable Expenses		
Salaries	$2,793,404	Includes hiring of two new full-time staff and average salary increase of 7% on eligible employees' anniversary date
Travel	180,991	Transportation, room, meals, and related expenses for staff and volunteers.
Printing	439,901	Increase of 62% due to producing a monthly rather than quarterly newsletter.
Postage	143,000	Increase of 20% due to mailing additional newsletters and postage rate increase.
Supplies	14,000	Consumable office supplies.
Telephone	83,500	Local and long-distance service.
Independent Contractors	80,000	Decrease due to hiring one full-time employee to replace an independent contractor. Independent contractors are primarily editors.
Miscellaneous	25,000	Self-explanatory.
Subtotal	$3,759,796	

Under Salaries:

	Current Employees	Projected Employees
	82 full-time	85 full-time
	7 part-time	7 part-time

Item	Proposed Budget	Explanation
Semi-Controllable Expenses		
Fringe Benefits	$371,379	Voluntary fringe benefits include the following:
Payroll Taxes	210,000	Statutory taxes include the following:
Other Taxes	75,000	Taxes include sales, real estate, and personal property.
Utilities	35,000	Utilities average $3.50 per square foot.

Fringe Benefits:
- ➢ Pension—6% of salary
- ➢ Health Insurance—Average $250 per employee

Payroll Taxes:
- ➢ Social Security
- ➢ Medicare
- ➢ Federal Unemployment
- ➢ State Unemployment

	EXHIBIT 15.1 *(Continued)*	
Item	**Proposed Budget**	**Explanation**
Semi-Controllable		
Expenses		
Insurance	$13,500	Insurance policies include the following:
		➤ Officers' and Directors' Liability
		➤ General Liability
		➤ Office Contents
		➤ Umbrella Policy
Subtotal	$704,879	
Fixed Expenses		
Rent	$380,000	We are in the third year of a five-year lease that ends December 31, 20X3. A lease escalation clause increased rent from $13.50 per square foot to $14.00 per square foot effective January 1, 20X1.
Interest	150,000	Current-year portion of notes payable at an average of 8%.
Lease Contracts	24,604	Leased computer equipment, copiers, and postage machine.
Maintenance Contracts	16,132	Maintenance on data processing equipment, copiers, and postage equipment.
Depreciation	26,939	Assets are depreciated on a straight-line basis.
Amortization	1,320	Fixed amortization on leasehold improvements.
Subtotal	$598,995	
Total Budgeted Expenses	$5,063,670	

EXHIBIT 15.1 *(Continued)*					
Five-Year Expense Trends and Fiscal Year 20X1 Budget					

	Audited Actuals					Budget
	20Y1	**20Y2**	**20Y3**	**20Y4**	**20X0**	**20X1**
Controllable Expenses						
Salaries	$1,967,531	$2,093,118	$2,226,721	$2,368,852	$2,520,056	$2,793,404
Travel	116,979	124,446	132,289	140,840	149,830	180,991
Printing	292,696	311,379	331,254	352,398	374,892	439,901
Postage	87,539	93,127	99,071	105,395	112,123	143,000
Supplies	9,720	10,340	11,001	11,703	12,450	14,000
Telephone	60,503	64,365	68,473	72,844	77,494	83,500
Independent Contractors	82,603	87,876	93,485	99,452	105,806	80,000
Miscellaneous	16,232	17,268	18,370	19,543	20,791	25,000
Subtotal	$2,633,803	$2,801,919	$2,980,764	$3,171,027	$3,373,436	$3,759,796
Semi-Controllable Expenses						
Fringe Benefits	$216,422	$230,236	$244,932	$260,566	$277,198	$371,379
Payroll Taxes	156,935	166,952	177,609	188,946	201,007	210,000
Other Taxes	53,651	57,076	60,719	64,595	68,719	75,000
Utilities	24,261	25,809	27,456	29,209	31,073	35,000
Insurance	9,603	10,216	10,868	11,562	12,300	13,500
Subtotal	$460,872	$490,289	$521,584	$554,878	$590,297	$704,879
Fixed Expenses						
Rent	$280,000	$300,000	$320,000	$340,000	$360,000	$380,000
Interest	171,351	169,009	167,800	165,900	160,800	150,000
Lease Contracts	20,003	20,793	22,604	22,604	24,624	24,624
Maintenance Contracts	11,090	13,500	13,500	14,906	15,648	16,132
Depreciation	19,606	20,005	21,907	22,654	24,540	26,939
Amortization	5,895	5,765	4,090	4,090	3,036	1,320
Subtotal	$507,945	$5,290,072	$549,901	$570,150	$588,648	$599,015
TOTALS	$3,602,620	$3,821,280	$4,052,249	$4,295,459	$4,552,381	$5,063,690

EXHIBIT 15.1 *(Continued)*

Fiscal Year 20X1 Budget Summary

			Percentage of Revenues
Revenues			
Dues		$3,694,172	71.5
Publication Sales	$755,557		
Less Cost of Goods Sold	(241,778)	513,779	9.9
Advertising		558,600	10.8
Interest		27,139	0.5
Conference			
Registration	275,000		
Exhibits	35,000	310,000	6.0
All Others		60,000	1.3
Total Revenues		$5,163,690	100.0

			Percentage of Expenses	
Expenses				
Controllable Expenses				
Salaries		$2,793,404	55.2	
Travel		180,991	3.6	
Printing		439,901	8.8	
Postage		143,000	2.8	
Supplies		14,000	0.3	
Telephone		83,500	1.7	
Independent Contractors		80,000	1.6	
Miscellaneous		25,000	0.6	
Subtotal		$3,759,796		74.6
Semi-Controllable Expenses				
Fringe Benefits		$371,379	7.3	
Payroll Taxes		210,000	4.1	
Other Taxes		75,000	1.5	
Utilities		35,000	0.7	
Insurance		13,500	0.3	
Subtotal		$704,879		13.9
Fixed Expenses				
Rent		$380,000	7.5	
Interest		150,000	2.7	
Lease Contracts		24,624	0.5	
Maintenance Contracts		16,132	0.3	
Depreciation		26,939	0.5	
Amortization		1,320		
Subtotal		$599,015		11.5
TOTAL EXPENSES		$5,063,690	100.0	100.0
Increase in Unrestricted Net Assets		$100,000		

EXHIBIT 15.1 *(Continued)*

20X1 Revenue Budget
$5,163,690

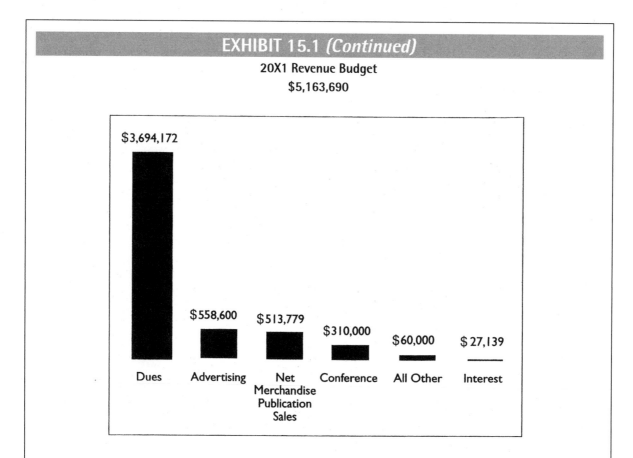

20X1 Expense Budget
$5,063,690

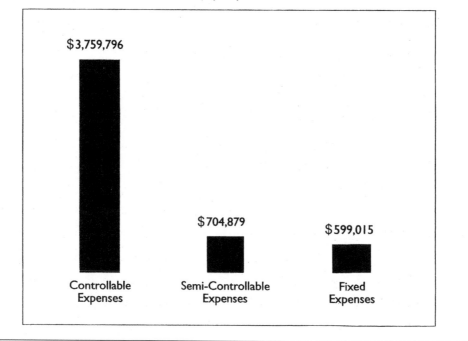

EXHIBIT 15.1 *(Continued)*

20X1 Revenue Budget
$5,163,690

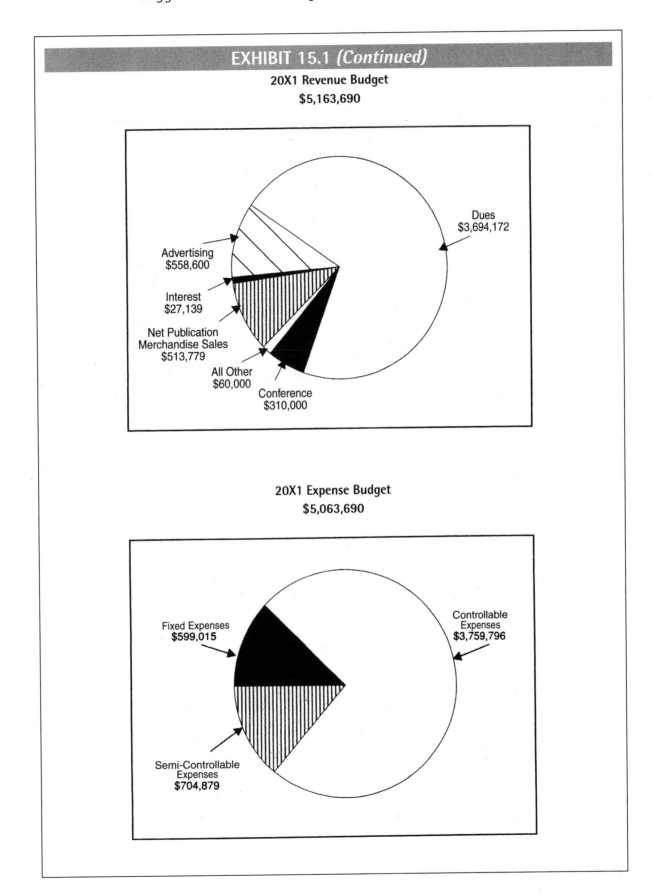

Dues
$3,694,172

Advertising
$558,600

Interest
$27,139

Net Publication
Merchandise Sales
$513,779

All Other
$60,000

Conference
$310,000

20X1 Expense Budget
$5,063,690

Controllable
Expenses
$3,759,796

Fixed Expenses
$599,015

Semi-Controllable
Expenses
$704,879

EXHIBIT 15.1 *(Continued)*

20X1 Budget Summary by Activity
Revenue Detail and Total Expenses

Department	Administration	Membership	Editorial	Conferences	Total
Revenues					
Dues	$	$3,694,172	$	$	$3,694,172
Publication Sales			755,557		755,557
Less Cost of Goods Sold			(241,778)		(241,778)
Advertising			558,600		558,600
Interest	27,139				27,139
Conferences					
Registration				275,000	275,000
Exhibits				35,000	35,000
All Other	60,000				60,000
Total Revenues	$87,139	$3,694,172	$1,072,379	$310,000	$5,163,690
Expenses					
Controllable	$736,014	$968,079	$1,522,891	$532,812	$3,759,796
Semi-Controllable	189,888	169,162	239,149	106,686	704,879
Fixed	272,291	102,985	160,279	63,460	599,015
Total Expenses	$1,198,193	$1,240,226	$1,922,319	$702,958	$5,063,690
Increase (Decrease)					
in Unrestricted					
Net Assets	($1,111,048)	$2,453,946	($849,940)	($392,958)	$100,000

EXHIBIT 15.1 *(Continued)*

20X1 Budget Summary by Activity
Total Revenues and Expense Detail

Department	Administration	Membership	Editorial	Conferences	Total
Total Revenues	$87,139	$3,694,172	$1,072,379	$310,000	$5,163,690
Expenses					
Controllable Expenses					
Salaries	$572,647	$703,938	$1,050,319	$466,500	$2,793,404
Travel	89,952	64,252	0	26,787	180,991
Printing	28,154	74,783	336,964	0	439,901
Postage	31,031	80,080	17,160	14,729	145,000
Supplies	3,640	5,880	1,708	2,772	14,000
Telephone	3,090	31,396	32,565	16,449	83,500
Independent Contractors	0	0	80,000	0	80,000
Miscellaneous	7,500	7,750	4,175	5,575	25,000
Subtotal	$736,014	$968,079	$1,522,891	$532,812	$3,759,796
Semi-Controllable Expenses					
Fringe Benefits	$76,132	$93,587	$139,639	$62,021	$371,379
Payroll Taxes	43,050	52,920	78,960	35,070	210,000
Other Taxes	50,025	13,800	7,425	3,750	75,000
Utilities	7,175	8,855	13,125	5,845	35,000
Insurance	13,500	0	0	0	13,500
Subtotal	$189,882	$169,162	$239,149	$106,686	$704,879
Fixed Expenses					
Rent	$77,900	$96,140	$142,500	$63,460	$380,000
Interest	150,000	0	0	0	150,000
Lease Contracts	0	6,845	17,779	0	24,624
Maintenance Contracts	16,132	0	0	0	16,132
Depreciation	26,939	0	0	0	26,939
Amortization	1,320	0	0	0	1,320
Subtotal	$272,291	$102,985	$160,279	$63,460	$599,015
Total Expenses	$1,198,187	$1,240,226	$1,922,319	$702,958	$5,063,690
Increase (Decrease) in Unrestricted Net Assets	($1,111,048)	$2,453,946	($849,940)	($392,958)	$100,000

EXHIBIT 15.1 *(Continued)*

20X1 Capital Acquisition Budget

The 20X1 budget includes the purchase of the following fixed assets:

Item	Purchase Date	Depreciation Cost	20X1 Method	Life	Depreciation
Conference Table	04/01	$5,000	Straight Line	10	$328
Personal Computer	06/01	4,000	Straight Line	5	462
Desk	07/01	2,000	Straight Line	10	96
Allowance for Unanticipated Purchases		8,600	Straight Line		200
Total Cash Outlay		$19,600	20X1 Depreciation Increase		$1,086
			Depreciation on assets purchased in prior years		$25,853
			Total 20X1 Depreciation		$26,939

EXHIBIT 15.1 (Continued)

20X1 Inventory Acquisition Budget

Item	Purchase Date	Total Cost	Purchase Quantity	Unit Cost	Selling Price	Projected Unit Sales	Projected Gross Sales	Cost of Goods Sold	Net Profit
Sweatshirts	01/04	$3,000	300	10	$15	1,000	$15,000	$10,000	$5,000
Jackets	06/01	6,000	500	12	20	500	10,000	6,000	4,000
New Publications	10/01	10,000	1,000	10	20	300	6,000	3,000	3,000
Total Cash Outlay		$19,000					$31,000	$19,000	$12,000

Gross Sales on 20X1 Inventory Purchases $31,000
Cost of Goods Sold (19,000)
Net Profit on 20X1 Inventory Purchases $12,000

EXHIBIT 15.1 (Continued)

Consolidated Cash Flow Budget
20X1

	Jan.	Feb.	Mar.	Apr.	May	Jun.	Jul.	Aug.	Sep.	Oct.	Nov.	Dec.
Cash Available, Beginning of Month	$101,323	$97,147	$117,992	$115,560	$102,679	$107,357	$98,720	$104,879	$106,725	$96,922	$115,914	$128,990
Plus Cash Received	59,409	69,940	73,123	47,120	93,010	81,981	72,205	73,911	51,513	69,069	68,088	70,047
Less Cash Disbursements	(63,585)	(49,095)	(75,555)	(60,001)	(88,332)	(90,618)	(66,046)	(72,065)	(61,316)	(50,077)	(55,012)	(62,709)
Equals Cash Available End of Month	$97,147	$117,992	$115,560	$102,679	$107,357	$98,720	$104,879	$106,725	$96,922	$115,914	$128,990	$136,328

16

The Role of the Budget Coordinator

A KEY TO THE SUCCESS or failure of the budget and financial management system is a competent budget coordinator. The person selected for this vital role should have a formal accounting background, a thorough understanding of technical areas (depreciation, taxes, and the like), and good organizational skills. In addition, the budget coordinator should have strong interpersonal skills, which will be required to coordinate the entire process with other staff members. The budget coordinator is responsible for the following:

➤ Distributing monthly financial statements, including budget detail, within 10 working days after the close of the prior month

➤ Coordinating and compiling approved monthly budgets submitted by other department managers into the master budget

➤ Reviewing capital expenditure requests

➤ Reviewing inventory purchase requests

➤ Analyzing monthly cash flow and project cash flow for the same month of the subsequent year

➤ Preparing the annual budget documents submitted to the approving body

➤ Serving as staff resource person for technical accounting and tax issues related to the budget

➤ Compiling the annual cash flow budget

Distributing Monthly Financial Statements

If the organization wants to take a proactive rather than a reactive position in addressing financial problems, financial statements must be accurate and be distributed after the close of every month. This is generally the responsibility of the budget coordinator.

Department financial statements include the detail of the original budget by line item. Budget detail can then be compared with the actual detail to implement true fiscal accountability.

Compiling the Master Budget

It is generally the responsibility of the budget coordinator to receive monthly budget data submitted by other department managers after they have been approved by the chief executive officer at the monthly budget meeting. These data are updated on the master budget for all departments for both the current month and the annual budget. Once the budget coordinator enters the data into the master budget, this information is returned to the submitting department to ensure accuracy and to correct any errors.

Reviewing Capital Expenditure Requests

Capital expenditure request forms completed by department managers must be reviewed by the budget coordinator. This review ensures that the cost is included in the cash flow budget and that depreciation is budgeted and calculated according to established policies.

Reviewing Inventory Purchase Requests

The inventory purchase request forms completed by department managers must be reviewed by the budget coordinator to ensure that the cash outlay is included in the cash flow budget.

Analyzing Cash Flow

The budget coordinator is responsible for analyzing where cash came from and where it went during the current month and must project sources and uses of cash for the same month of the subsequent year. These projections are based on the adjusted monthly budgets submitted by other managers.

Preparing Annual Budget Documents

The budget coordinator is responsible for preparing the final budget documents that will be sent to the approving body. These documents include the following:

➤ Detailed explanation of all revenues and expenses

➤ Revenues and expense trends for five years

➤ The capital purchases budget

➤ The inventory acquisition budget

➤ The cash flow budget

Advising on Accounting and Tax Issues

Department managers should not be burdened with budgeting for items outside their control. However, someone has to take that responsibility and, logically, that person is most likely the budget coordinator. To perform this task, the budget coordinator should have an accounting background and a thorough understanding of technical areas, such as fringe benefits and payroll taxes; depreciation and amortization; and federal, state, and local taxes.

In addition, the budget coordinator is responsible for accurately budgeting all semi-controllable and fixed expenses, including the following:

➤ Rent and rent increases

➤ Lease obligations

➤ Utilities

➤ Maintenance contracts

➤ Insurance premiums

➤ Interest expense

Compiling Annual Cash Flow Budget

Another technical responsibility of the budget coordinator is compiling cash flow data. If the organization wants to maximize investment opportunity and ensure that cash is available for routine operations, a cash flow budget is necessary. When the cash flow budget is prepared accurately, the investment decisions should be made according to established organization policy.

CHAPTER 17

Accounting and Budgeting for Fringe Benefits

FRINGE BENEFITS ARE DIFFICULT items for which to account and budget. Because they are a semi-controllable expense, the budget coordinator should be responsible for budgeting for fringe benefits.

Although accurate accounting and reporting should be the goal of every financial budget system, accounting for and allocating fringe benefits precisely to individual departments is complicated, time consuming, and generally inaccurate. One way to simplify the process is to charge all fringe benefits to one clearing account and to charge each department a share of the monthly fringe benefits corresponding to the share of salaries charged to each department (Exhibit 17.1).

The first step in this process is to define fringe benefits. Fringe benefits should be related directly to salary and should not include items such as company cars, educational reimbursement, and other employment-related perquisites. The following are typical items considered to be fringe benefits:

Statutory	Voluntary
FICA	Pension
Medicare	Life insurance
State unemployment	Health insurance
FUTA	Disability insurance
Workers' compensation insurance	Dental insurance
	Day care

Budgeting for fringe benefits is easy if the organization uses the clearing account method and properly defines fringe benefits. With this system, the percentages used in budget calculations will change only if new fringe benefits are added or if individual fringe benefit item percentages change.

EXHIBIT 17.1

Examples of Fringe Benefits Allocation

Total Fringe Benefits Paid
Month of February 20X0

Item	Amount
FICA	$2,387
Medicare	444
State Unemployment	185
FUTA	
Workers' Compensation	300
Pension	2,400
Life Insurance	200
Health Insurance	2,500
Disability Insurance	100
Dental Insurance	300
Day Care	750
TOTAL	**$9,566**

Salaries by Department		Salary % by Department	Fringe Benefits Charged
Administration	$10,000	27.0	$2,583 ($9,566 × 27.0%)
Membership	14,000	37.8	3,616 ($9,566 × 37.8%)
Editorial	7,000	18.9	1,808 ($9,566 × 18.9%)
Training	6,000	16.3	1,559 ($9,566 × 16.3%)
TOTAL	**$37,000**	**100.0**	**$9,566**

Fringe Benefits as a Percentage of Salary, Month of February 20X0.

$$\$9,566 \div \$37,000 = \underline{\underline{25.85\%}}$$

Fringe Benefits as a Percentage of Salary, Year to Date = $\underline{\underline{24.83\%}}$

18

The Capital Budget and Depreciation

A CAPITAL BUDGET is necessary to determine whether enough cash is available to purchase an asset or whether a loan is necessary. In addition, capital budgets must be prepared to ensure that the depreciation expense is budgeted for properly. If an organization has good records of fixed assets and depreciation, prepares a capital budget, and does not purchase unbudgeted assets, depreciation expense should be exactly predictable.

As part of the monthly budgeting process, managers complete capital expenditure request forms when new equipment is needed. The form should be designed to give the budget coordinator the information needed to forecast the basis for depreciation separated from items to be expensed when paid. In addition, capital purchases affect the organization's cash flow budget.

Whether an asset should be capitalized or expensed is determined by the answers to two questions:

➢ Is the useful life of the item purchased greater than one year?

➢ Does the cost of the item exceed the capitalization cutoff point?

The capitalization cutoff point is the dollar figure under which an item is expensed in the period purchased and over which it will be capitalized and depreciated for the length of its useful life.

If an item is capitalized, it will be recorded among the fixed assets of the organization and depreciated in accordance with the organization's depreciation policy. Depreciation methods include the following:

➢ Modified accelerated cost recovery system (MACRS)

➢ Accelerated cost recovery system (ACRS)

➢ Straight line

➤ Sum of the year's digits

➤ Double declining balance

➤ Income forecasting

Depreciation methods other than straight line are considered accelerated. The most common depreciation methods used today by not-for-profit organizations are MACRS and straight line. In straight-line depreciation, the same amount of depreciation is recorded every period. In accelerated depreciation, however, the amount of depreciation recorded is more in the earlier years and declines steadily thereafter.

Common Depreciation Method Formulas for Not–for–Profit Organizations

Straight Line

$$(\text{Cost} - \text{Salvage Value}) \div \text{Useful Life} = \text{Depreciation per Period}$$

If an organization uses the straight-line method for depreciating assets, electronic equipment purchases should be depreciated over a five-year period to avoid absorbing several years' depreciation in one period because of unplanned obsolescence.

MACRS

MACRS is a depreciation method in which allowable percentages of depreciation per year have been assigned by the Internal Revenue Service. Most office equipment will be depreciated according to the following percentages if factors such as midquarter conversion do not apply:

Year 1	Year 2	Year 3	Year 4	Year 5	Year 6
20%	32%	19.2%	11%	11.52%	5.76%

Capital Expenditure Request Forms

The budget coordinator calculates depreciation expense and the effect of capital purchases on cash flow based on completed capital expenditure request forms (Exhibit 18.1) submitted by managers. Depreciation expense is entered into the master budget, and capital purchases are entered into the organization's record of fixed assets and depreciation schedule. An example of a record of fixed assets and depreciation schedule is shown in Exhibit 18.2.

A summary of the current-year capital budget—along with a detail of items purchased, effect on cash flow, and resulting depreciation—should be included with the budget documents sent to the approving body.

EXHIBIT 18.1

Sample Form for Capital Expenditure Request

Capital Expenditure Request

Item(s) Requested_____

_____

Is equipment new_____or replacement equipment_____?

If replacement equipment, describe old equipment_____

_____

_____

Intended purchase date_____

Anticipated Costs:

Equipment	$_____	Start-up Supplies	$_____
Installation	_____	Maintenance Contract	_____
Sales Tax	_____	Other	
Shipping	_____	_____	_____
Insurance on Shipping	_____	_____	_____
TOTAL	$_____	TOTAL	$_____

EXHIBIT 18.2

Sample Record of Fixed Assets and Depreciation Schedule

Record of Fixed Assets and Depreciation Schedule

Date Purchased	Item	Depreciation Cost	Method	Life	20Y1 Actual	20Y2 Actual	20X0 Actual	20X1 Budget
20Y1	Conference Table	$10,000	SL	10	$1,000	$1,000	$1,000	$1,000
20Y1	Office Furniture	12,000	SL	10	1,200	1,200	1,200	1,200
20Y1	Word Processor	8,000	SL	5	1,600	1,600	1,600	1,600
20Y1	1 Desk	1,200	SL	10	120	120	120	120
20Y2	1 Desk	1,300	SL	10		130	130	130
20Y2	4 Chairs	800	SL	10		80	80	80
20Y2	10 File Cabinets	900	SL	10		90	90	90
20Y2	Safe	2,000	SL	10		200	200	200
20X0	Computer	5,000	SL	5			1,000	1,000
20X0	Printer	2,000	SL	5			400	400
Subtotal		$43,200			$3,920	$4,420	$5,820	$5,820
20X1 Capital Budget								
	Postage Equip.	$6,000	SL	5				$1,200
	Copier	10,000	SL	5				2,000
	Desk	1,100	SL	10				110
Total		$60,300				20X1 Depreciation Budget		$9,130

CHAPTER 19

Inventory Purchases and Calculation of Cost of Goods Sold

IT IS IMPORTANT to budget accurately for resale publication purchases and resale merchandise purchases because they directly affect the cash flow budget and calculation of cost of goods sold. As with capital purchases, managers complete an inventory purchase request (Exhibit 19.1) as part of their monthly budgeting responsibilities. The form should be designed to give the budget coordinator information for computing the cost of goods sold and the effects of inventory purchases on cash flow.

Effect on the Cash Flow Budget

Purchases of publications and other items that will be held for resale must be budgeted separately by item because the purchases will tie up available cash for an extended period. This budgeting method is particularly important if the organization wants to ensure that cash is available to meet current obligations and to maximize investment earnings.

Calculation of Cost of Goods Sold

Separate cost of goods sold calculations should be made for each item held for resale, rather than applying one cost of goods sold percentage to gross sales. The totals for all cost of goods sold calculations identify both the overall cost of goods sold for the entire organization and an overall gross profit percentage.

Assuming the organization uses the continuous budget method, and the preliminary budget for the same month of the subsequent year is approved at the monthly budget meeting, the inventory purchase requests are sent to the budget coordinator for the cash flow budget. A summary of the current year's inventory purchases, effects on cash flow, projected sales, and projected profits should be included with the budget documents forwarded to the approving body.

EXHIBIT 19.1

Sample Form for Inventory Purchase Request

Inventory Purchase Request

Name of Item   _____

Intended Purchase Date   _____

Costs

    Printing $_____

    Typesetting   _____

    Freight   _____

    Insurance   _____

Total Cash Required $_____

Cost of Goods Sold Calculations

Total Cash Required	Quantity Purchased	Unit Cost of Goods Sold
$	÷	= $_____

Gross Profit per Unit

Selling Price per Unit	Unit Cost of Goods Sold	Gross Profit per Unit
$	−	= $_____

Gross Profit Percentage

Gross Profit	Selling Price	Gross Profit %
$	÷	$ =_____%

CHAPTER 20

Accounting and Budgeting for Dues

ALTHOUGH DUES ARE the lifeblood of membership organizations and are typically the primary source of revenue, they often are not accounted for properly. Two common, major accounting errors regarding dues must be addressed if an organization wants a proper, meaningful, and understandable accounting statement presentation:

➤ Treating uncollected dues as an account receivable on the Statement of Financial Position

➤ Failing to use the deferral method of accounting for dues revenue

The first problem, treating uncollected dues as an account receivable, occurs when the organization sends out its membership dues renewal invoices and books the total as an account receivable and corresponding dues revenue in the accounting records. As members renew, the cash is used to reduce the accounts receivable balance. This method of accounting for uncollected dues is dangerous and often results in audit adjustments by the independent CPA firm. These adjustments could be embarrassing if management has been reporting incorrect financial data.

Independent CPA firms must assure themselves according to Generally Accepted Auditing Standards that the accounts receivable are valid. To do this, the accountants must decide whether the members have a legal obligation to remit payment. This is almost never the case, because dues renewal invoices are merely requests for members to rejoin the organization. No legal contract exists, and because the organization has no legal right to pursue collection, the accountants have no choice but to remove these receivables from the financial records.

If accounts receivable for uncollected dues are removed from the accounting records, the corresponding dues revenue on the statement will also be reduced. This usually results in audited financial statements that are materially different from financial statements prepared internally.

The second problem, failing to use the deferral system of accounting for dues revenue, occurs when the total dues collected in a given month is recorded as dues revenue in that month. Typically, dues represent an entire year's worth of membership services. If dues are recorded as revenue when collected, the financial statements for that month will be overstated and misleading. When financial statements reflect an inflated excess of revenues over expenses, decisions based on the inflated figures will likely have negative consequences because they will be based on inaccurate financial data.

Accrual accounting does not record income until it is earned. Because monthly membership services expenses are associated with an annual dues payment, an attempt should be made to match revenues with corresponding expenses by deferring revenues until they have been earned.

While deferring dues may sound complex, it is actually simple, and is illustrated in the following example.

Assume a not-for-profit organization bills for $150,000 in dues in January but receives only $120,000 in cash. How much dues revenue is recorded in January? The answer is simple: $10,000 ($120,000 divided by 12 months). The remaining $110,000 is recorded as deferred income (a liability account) on the Statement of Financial Position.

How much dues revenue is recorded in February if the same organization bills for $75,000 in February but collects only $60,000? The answer is $15,000 (the $60,000 collected in February divided by 12 months equals $5,000 to be recognized in February in addition to the $10,000 deferred from January; the remaining $55,000 of February dues is deferred for the next 11 months).

This idea is clearer when the same figures are illustrated in a deferred dues schedule (Exhibit 20.1). In this example, $10,000 of $120,000 collected in January is recognized as dues revenue, and the remaining $110,000 is deferred for the next 11 months. In February, $5,000 of $60,000 collected in February is recognized as dues revenue and added to the $10,000 deferred from January, resulting in $15,000 of dues revenue to be recognized in February. The February year-to-date income statements would show $25,000 in dues revenue, and the Statement of Financial Position would show a deferred dues liability of $155,000.

Deferred dues are considered a liability on the financial statements for the following reasons:

➢ A liability exists to provide future membership services.

➢ There is an actual cash liability to refund a prorated share of unused dues to members when requested.

EXHIBIT 20.1

Sample Deferred Dues Schedule

Dues Collected	Jan.	Feb.	Mar.	Apr.	May	Jun.	Jul.	Aug.	Sep.	Oct.	Nov.	Dec.	Jan.
January $120,000	$10,000	$10,000	$10,000	$10,000	$10,000	$10,000	$10,000	$10,000	$10,000	$10,000	$10,000	$10,000	——
February $60,000	——	5,000 $15,000	5,000	5,000	5,000	5,000	5,000	5,000	5,000	5,000	5,000	5,000	$5,000

Note: The double-underlined figures represent the actual amount of dues revenue recorded in the financial statements.

Budgeting for Dues

Proper budgeting for dues is based on three assumptions:

➤ Uncollected dues are not recorded as accounts receivable.

➤ The organization uses the deferral method of accounting for dues revenue.

➤ The organization uses the continuous budget method.

Once the monthly financial statements have been distributed, the person responsible for dues analyzes actual cash collected. The cash collected is the basis for the dues revenue budget.

The person responsible for dues should have a thorough understanding of the deferral method of accounting for dues revenue and should communicate this understanding to everyone involved in the dues collection. In addition, the person responsible for budgeting for cash collections on dues can now prepare the dues revenue budget.

Once the current-month data have been analyzed, the subsequent-year prediction for cash collected for dues is adjusted by upper management. Once the adjustment has been implemented, the amount of dues revenue to be budgeted is computed from the budgeted deferred dues schedule.

In Exhibit 20.2, the Membership Department budgeted cash collections for dues in the amounts of $24,000, $6,000, and $12,000 for January, February, and March, respectively. These amounts are divided by 12 and added to the prior deferred dues amounts to arrive at the dues revenue budget for each month. The budgeted cash collections are forwarded to the budget coordinator and used to compute the cash flow budget.

EXHIBIT 20.2

Sample Budget Deferred Dues Schedule

Budget Deferred Dues Schedule

	Jan.	Feb.	Mar.	Apr.	May	Jun.	Jul.	Aug.	Sep.	Oct.	Nov.	Dec.
Deferred Dues Totals												
Actual from Prior Year	$20,000	$19,000	$17,000	$16,000	$14,000	$10,000	$9,000	$7,000	$6,000	$4,000	$3,000	$1,000
Budgeted Cash Collections												
January $24,000	2,000 / $22,000	2,000	2,000	2,000	2,000	2,000	2,000	2,000	2,000	2,000	2,000	2,000
February $6,000		500 / $21,500	500	500	500	500	500	500	500	500	500	500
March $12,000			$1,000 / $20,500	1,000	1,000	1,000	1,000	1,000	1,000	1,000	1,000	1,000
Etc.												

Note: The budgeted cash collections are divided by 12, allocated to the proper 12 months, and added to the prior deferred dues amounts to arrive at the dues revenue budget for each month (the double-underlined figures).

CHAPTER 21

Capital Assets: Lease-or-Buy Decisions

LEASE-OR-BUY DECISIONS of commercial organizations usually are motivated by tax implications. Not-for-profit organizations, however, generally base lease-or-buy decisions on cash position.

There are two types of leases: operating leases and capital leases. An operating lease is one that does not meet capital lease criteria. It is an ongoing-expense line item on the Statement of Activity, and the equipment is not included among fixed assets on the Statement of Financial Position.

A capital lease is one that records the asset among fixed assets on the Statement of Financial Position and as a corresponding liability. The asset is depreciated over the shorter of its useful life and its lease term, rather than expensed as a line item on the expense statement as payments are made.

A lease must be a capital lease if any one of the following criteria is met:

➤ It has a bargain buyout (purchase) option (for example, if at the end of the lease the equipment can be purchased for a nominal fee).

➤ Ownership is automatically transferred to the lessee at end of the lease term.

➤ The lease term is 75 percent or more of estimated useful life.

➤ The present value of a minimum lease payment is greater than or equal to 90 percent of the fair market value of the leased property.

Generally, an item is more likely to be purchased outright, or the organization will enter into a capital lease, if the item is critical equipment and it is desirable to keep the asset after the lease terminates. Typical capital lease items include computers and copiers.

Generally, an organization is more likely to enter into an operating lease if it intends to use the equipment for a short time. Typical operating lease items include company cars and postage equipment.

An organization must read the lease carefully when budgeting for leases, whether operating or capital. It is common for the leasing company to pass on responsibility for paying property taxes to the lessee; these taxes can be substantial and must be budgeted for. Also, it is important not to include capital lease items on the reports sent to departments of assessment and taxation, to avoid paying personal property taxes twice.

CHAPTER 22

The Long–Range Plan

LONG–RANGE PLANS are for five or more years. Formal long-range plans are essential to the financial health and future of an organization, and it is important to understand how long-range plans integrate with the current-year budget.

A long-range plan is the strategy for the future. The plan states broad objectives for the organization, and management usually is responsible for projecting how these broad goals will be accomplished financially. Broad goals that should be considered include the following:

➢ Industry trends

➢ Inflation factors

➢ New programs

➢ Elimination of programs

➢ Capital purchases

➢ Inventory purchases

➢ Long-range financial objectives

➢ Cash flow projections

Long-range plans are also called strategic plans and should be integrated with the goals of the current-year budget, also called the tactical plan. These financial goals are components that help determine where the organization desires its unrestricted net assets to be at certain future dates. The relationship between long-range plans and current-year budgets should be systematic and integrated.

The integration process involves the following steps:

1. Top management specifies broad long-range objectives.

2. Functional managers develop their own budget segments of these broad goals.

3. Functional budgets are reviewed, evaluated, and revised.

4. Revised functional budgets are consolidated into the master long-range plan.

The long-range plan's financial goals should be integrated into formal current-year budget documents to emphasize that the current-year budget meets these goals. Long-range plans should be updated annually as with the continuous monthly budget update system. Annual updates avoid time-consuming long-range plan preparations. In addition, long-range plans should consider the importance of attempting to plan for diversifying revenue sources. Obviously, any organization that relies too heavily on one revenue source will face difficult budget adjustments if economic factors negatively affect that one revenue source.

CHAPTER 23

Financial Ratios

THERE ARE MANY financial ratios used primarily by lending institutions and investors. Most of these ratios are of little or no use to budget preparers. However, seven ratios should be addressed when examining financial statements, reviewing the budget, and using the cash flow budget.

Statement of Financial Position Ratios:

➢ Current ratio

➢ Acid test ratio

Sales and Profits Ratios:

➢ Asset earning power ratio

➢ Return on equity ratio

➢ Net profit on sales ratio

➢ Investment turnover ratio

➢ Return on investment (ROI) ratio

Statement of Financial Position Ratios

Current Ratio

The current ratio is an important measure of financial stability, and it asks the question, "Does the organization possess enough current assets to pay its current debts?"

Total Current Assets ÷ Total Current Liabilities = Current Ratio

For example, if an organization's total current assets are $150,000 and current liabilities are $50,000, the ratio is computed as follows:

$$\frac{\$150{,}000}{\text{(Current Assets)}} \div \frac{\$50{,}000}{\text{(Current Liabilities)}} = \frac{3.1}{\text{(Current Ratio, also expressed as 3 to 1 or 3:1)}}$$

What is a good current ratio? This question cannot be answered with an exact figure, but a popular rule of thumb is to strive for a current ratio of 2 to 1. This, of course, depends on the specific nature and characteristics of the organization.

Acid Test Ratio

The acid test ratio, also known as the quick ratio, is the best measure of immediate liquidity.

$$\text{(Cash + Cash Equivalents)} \div \text{(Current Liabilities)} = \text{Acid Test Ratio}$$

The acid test ratio is much more precise than the current ratio. It addresses the organization's ability to pay its current obligations in case of declining revenues, poor accounts receivable collections, or other difficulties. For example, if an organization has cash on hand in the amount of $200,000 and government securities in the amount of $50,000 and its current liabilities total $125,000, the ratio would be computed as follows:

$$\frac{\$200{,}000}{\text{(Cash)}} + \frac{\$50{,}000}{\text{(Cash Equivalents)}} = \frac{\$250{,}000}{\text{(Cash plus Cash Equivalents)}}$$

$$\$250{,}000 \text{ (Cash plus Cash Equivalents)} \div \$125{,}000 \text{ (Current Liabilities)} =$$

$$\frac{2.1}{\text{(Acid-Test Ratio, also expressed as 2 to 1 or 2:1)}}$$

What is a good acid test ratio? Again, this question cannot be answered with exact figures, but the rule of thumb is that 1 to 1 is satisfactory.

Sales and Profits Ratios

Although there are rules of thumb to apply to Statement of Financial Position ratios, similar rules do not apply to ratios based on sales and profits because of the considerable differences among enterprises.

Asset Earning Power Ratio

The asset earning power ratio is a good indication of the total earning power of the organization without regard to creditor obligations, organizational equity, taxes, and so forth.

$$\text{Operating Profits} \div \text{Total Assets} = \text{Asset Earning Power}$$

The ratio usually is expressed as a percentage. For example, if operating profits are $50,000 and total assets are $250,000, the asset earning power is computed as follows:

$$\frac{\$50,000}{\text{(Operating Profits)}} \div \frac{\$250,000}{\text{(Total Assets)}} = \frac{20\%}{\text{(Asset Earning Power)}}$$

Return on Equity Ratio

The return on equity ratio suggests the return received on business investment, and generally the 12-month average method is used.

$$\text{Net Profit} \div \text{Equity} = \text{Return on Equity Ratio}$$

The ratio is usually expressed as a percentage. For example, if net profits are $30,000 and equity totals $90,000, the return on equity ratio is computed as follows:

$$\frac{\$30,000}{\text{(Net Profit)}} \div \frac{\$90,000}{\text{(Equity)}} = \frac{33\%}{\text{(Return on Equity Ratio)}}$$

Net Profit on Sales Ratio

This net profit on sales ratio shows the difference between what an organization receives in sales and what it spends. It can be computed in two ways:

➢ Net profit on gross sales

➢ Net profit on net sales

The net profit on gross sales is computed before deducting the cost of goods sold.

$$\text{Net Profit} \div \text{Gross Sales} = \text{Net Profit on Gross Sales Ratio}$$

The ratio usually is expressed as a percentage. For example, if an organization grosses $500,000 before deducting cost of goods sold and the total net profit is $50,000, the computation would be as follows:

$$\frac{\$50,000}{\text{(Net Profit)}} \div \frac{\$500,000}{\text{(Gross Sales)}} = \frac{10\%}{\text{(Net Profit on Gross Sales Ratio)}}$$

If the same organization wants to measure net profit on net sales, it would deduct the cost of goods sold from gross sales and divide this figure by the net profit:

	Gross Sales	$500,000
−	Cost of Goods Sold	−300,000
=	Net Sales	$200,000

The net profit on net sales would now be computed as follows:

$$\frac{\$50,000}{\text{(Net Profit)}} \div \frac{\$200,000}{\text{(Net Sales)}} = \frac{25\%}{\text{(Net Profit on Net Sales Ratio)}}$$

Investment Turnover Ratio

The investment turnover ratio computes the ratio between annual net sales and total investment and shows the volume of sales each dollar invested in assets produces.

Annual Net Sales ÷ Investment = Investment Turnover Ratio

For example, if an organization's annual net sales are $750,000 and its total investment is $75,000, the investment turnover ratio would be computed as follows:

$$\frac{\$750,000}{\text{(Annual Net Sales)}} \div \frac{\$75,000}{\text{(Total Investment)}} = \frac{10 \text{ Times}}{\text{(Investment Turnover Ratio)}}$$

Return on Investment Ratio

The ROI ratio also can be computed in one of two ways:

➤ Profits ÷ Equity = ROI Ratio

➤ Profits ÷ Total Assets = ROI Ratio

The ratio is usually expressed as a percentage. For example, if an organization wishes to measure ROI on equity and its equity is $50,000 and profits are $10,000, the ROI ratio would be computed as follows:

$$\frac{\$10,000}{\text{(Profits)}} \div \frac{\$50,000}{\text{(Equity)}} = \frac{20\%}{\text{(ROI Ratio)}}$$

If the same organization wishes to measure ROI on total assets and total assets are $200,000, the ROI ratio would be computed as follows:

$$\frac{\$10,000}{\text{(Profits)}} \div \frac{\$200,000}{\text{(Total Assets)}} = \frac{5\%}{\text{(ROI Ratio)}}$$

CHAPTER 24

Zero-Based Budgeting

IN ZERO-BASED BUDGETING, the history of actual revenues and expenses is not used as a reference for a new budget. The continued existence of programs must be justified from both the financial and the operational perspectives before the programs are included in the new budget. In other words, the budget starts at zero.

Zero-based budgeting was established as an attempt to revamp the outdated budgeting process of reviewing the revenue and expense history of the prior period, adjusting it for inflation and salary increases, and living with it. This old budgeting process is easy, but it does not address important issues, such as fiscal accountability, evaluation of program effectiveness, and evaluation of resource allocation.

A zero-based budgeting system has four components:

1. Operational goals are established and prioritized.

2. The costs of attaining these goals are projected. (Note that the actual prior financial costs associated with continuing programs are not used as a base or reference.)

3. Goals are ranked in order of importance to the organization.

4. The continuation of existing programs, the establishment of new programs, and the elimination of any unjustified existing programs are decided during budget approval.

Zero-based budgeting systems have certain advantages that should benefit the entire organization:

➤ Budgets are prepared with far more accuracy and detail.

➤ Resources are allocated in a systematic, well-thought-out manner.

➤ Organizational goals are reviewed and prioritized continually.

➤ Unjustified programs are eliminated.

However, zero-based budgeting systems have significant disadvantages:

➤ Significantly more budget preparation time is required to prepare justification for activities. This time could be spent on more productive activities.

➤ Organizations should have an operational goal of reducing paperwork. In a zero-based budgeting system, the required budget paperwork can be voluminous.

➤ Prioritizing goals and programs requires a significant amount of management time and could result in unwanted managerial competition, decreased employee morale, and other problems.

CHAPTER 25

Putting It All Together

THIS HANDBOOK ADDRESSES in detail every important component of an association's operating budget. This chapter illustrates how a typical month's budget may be compiled by:

➤ Completing the budget forms distributed to the membership manager as discussed in Chapter 12

➤ Assuming the role of the budget coordinator by budgeting for the semi-controllable and fixed expenses relating to the membership budget for the same month

➤ Illustrating the budget detail, including all revenues and expenses associated with the membership department, for the same month of the subsequent year

In Chapter 12, the membership manager received the two-month financial statement for the membership department along with a memorandum from the chief staff executive instructing the membership manager to complete the following:

➤ The analysis of current-month data form

➤ The monthly report on activities

➤ The subsequent-year budget projection form

➤ An inventory purchase request

➤ A capital expenditure request

➤ An expense reduction plan

Copies of the memorandum and financial statement are repeated on the following pages (Exhibits 25.1 and 25.2). Forms completed by the membership manager follow the financial statement (Exhibits 25.3 through 25.8).

EXHIBIT 25.1

Sample Memorandum of Instructions

To: Membership Manager
From: Chief Executive Officer
Date: March 10, 20X0
Re: Financial Statements/Continuous Budget

Attached are the Membership Department's financial statements for the two-month period ending February 28, 20X0. Be advised that the monthly budget meeting is scheduled for March 15, 20X0, at 10:00 A.M. You should be prepared to bring the following:

➢ A completed analysis of current-month data
➢ A completed monthly report on activities
➢ A completed subsequent-year budget projection
➢ A completed inventory purchase request
➢ A completed capital expenditure request
➢ A completed expense reduction plan

EXHIBIT 25.2

Sample Statement of Activity for Membership Department

Statement of Activity—Membership Department
For the Two-Month Period Ended February 28, 20X0

	Current Month					Year to Date				Total Current
Prior Year Actual	Current Year Budget	Current Year Actual	Variance			Prior Year Actual	Current Year Budget	Current Year Actual	Variance	Current Year Budget
					Revenues					
$268,308	$275,000	$278,050	$3,050		Dues	$540,626	$575,134	$576,398	$1,264	$3,358,388
					Expenses					
					Controllable Expenses					
$67,680	$72,000	$71,383	$617		Salaries	$95,880	$102,000	$102,766	($766)	$641,243
920	1,000	1,003	(3)		Travel	9,049	9,500	9,050	450	53,543
5,344	5,500	5,308	192		Printing	9,944	10,600	10,405	195	62,400
3,906	4,100	4,156	(56)		Postage	9,568	10,000	10,093	(93)	61,600
427	450	421	29		Supplies	839	875	871	4	5,166
471	500	491	9		Telephone	4,098	4,250	4,600	(350)	28,200
					Miscellaneous					
483	500	485	15		Expenses	902	975	1,002	(27)	5,968
$79,231	$84,050	$83,247	$803		Subtotal	$130,280	$138,200	$138,787	($587)	$858,120
					Semi-Controllable Expenses					
$9,292	$10,000	$9,969	$31		Fringe Benefits	$10,921	$11,618	$11,584	$34	$69,486
6,110	6,500	6,686	(186)		Payroll Taxes	7,789	8,286	8,448	(162)	50,434
1,599	1,760	1,850	(90)		Other Taxes	1,898	1,989	2,042	(53)	12,441
607	675	684	(9)		Utilities	1,206	1,300	1,227	73	7,590
$17,608	$18,935	$19,189	($254)		Subtotal	$21,814	$23,193	$23,301	($108)	$139,951
					Fixed Expenses					
$4,700	$5,000	$5,000	$0		Rent	$14,269	$15,180	$15,180	$0	$91,080
550	570	570	0		Lease Contracts	1,101	1,140	1,140	0	6,845
$5,250	$5,570	$5,570	$0		Subtotal	$15,370	$16,320	$16,320	$0	$97,925
$102,089	$108,555	$108,006	$549		**Total Expenses**	$167,464	$177,713	$178,408	($695)	$1,095,996
					Increase (Decrease) in Unrestricted					
$166,219	$166,445	$170,044	$3,599		**Net Assets**	$373,162	$397,421	$397,990	$569	$2,262,392

EXHIBIT 25.3

Sample Form for Analysis of Current-Month Data

Analysis of Current-Month Data
Membership Department
February 28, 20X0

After each item, provide a detailed analysis of actual figures for the current month and an explanation of variances.

	Budget	Actual	Variance
Revenues: Dues	$275,000	$278,050	($3,050)

210	New members @ $300 ea.	= 63,000
632	Renewal members @ $300 ea.	= 189,600
25	Associate members @ $400 ea.	= 10,000
103	Student members @ $150 ea.	= 15,450

	Budget	Actual	Variance
Controllable Expenses: Salaries	$72,000	$71,383	$617

			Leave Hours		
Employee Name	Regular Wages	Overtime Wages	Annual	Sick	Personal
Membership Mgr.	$8,000	—	—	—	—
Asst. Mgr.	$6,000	—	40	—	—
Admin. ass't.	$5,500	—	—	16	—
Clerks	$45,000	$6,883	120	56	12

Overtime necessary to process unexpected new members.

	Budget	Actual	Variance
Travel	$1,000	$1,003	($3)

Trip to Washington, D.C., to attend membership marketing seminar.	
Airfare	$550
Lodging and Meals	$453

EXHIBIT 25.3 *(Continued)*

	Budget	Actual	Variance
Printing	$5,500	$5,308	$192

Full-color membership recruitment brochure.

3,000 copies printed @ a unit cost of $1.77 each.

	Budget	Actual	Variance
Postage	$4,100	$4,156	($56)

Postage to mail membership recruitment brochure: $3,152

Regular postage: $1,004

	Budget	Actual	Variance
Supplies	$450	$421	$29

Routine office supplies

	Budget	Actual	Variance
Telephone	$500	$491	$9

Local service $200

Long distance $291

	Budget	Actual	Variance
Miscellaneous	$500	$485	$15

Expenses incurred to take membership committee to

dinner after annual meeting.

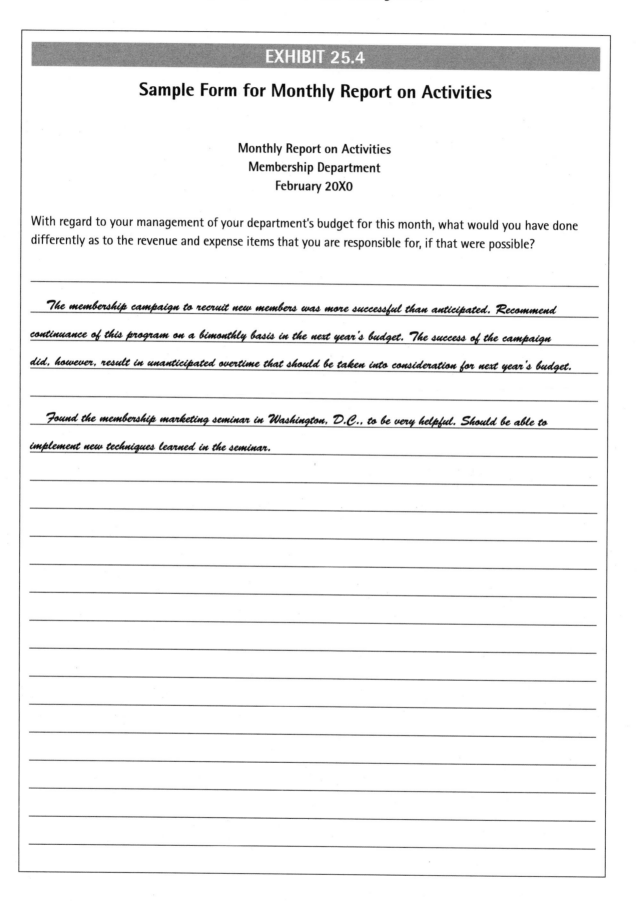

EXHIBIT 25.4

Sample Form for Monthly Report on Activities

Monthly Report on Activities
Membership Department
February 20X0

With regard to your management of your department's budget for this month, what would you have done differently as to the revenue and expense items that you are responsible for, if that were possible?

The membership campaign to recruit new members was more successful than anticipated. Recommend continuance of this program on a bimonthly basis in the next year's budget. The success of the campaign did, however, result in unanticipated overtime that should be taken into consideration for next year's budget.

Found the membership marketing seminar in Washington, D.C., to be very helpful. Should be able to implement new techniques learned in the seminar.

EXHIBIT 25.5

Sample Form for Subsequent-Year Budget Projection

Subsequent-Year Budget Projection
Membership Department
February 20X1

Based on your analysis of actual data for the month of February 20X0, detail and explain your predictions for the same revenues and expenses for February 20X1.

	Actual Feb. 20X0	Budget Feb. 20X1
Revenues: Dues	$278,050	$300,750

250 New members @ $300 ea. = $75,000

650 Renewal members @ 300 ea. = 195,000

30 Associate members @ 400 ea. = 12,000

125 Student members @ 150 ea. = 18,750

Are there any revenue items not listed that will be credited to the Membership Department in February 20X1? Explain and budget accordingly.

	Budget Feb. 20X1
Item: <u>Affinity Credit Card</u>	$500

Anticipated royalty from credit card offering to members.

	Actual Feb. 20X0	Budget Feb. 20X1
Total Revenues	$278,050	$301,250

EXHIBIT 25.5 *(Continued)*

Expenses

Salaries

	Actual Feb. 20X0 $71,383		Budget Feb. 20X1 $79,500	
Employee Name	Regular Wages	Overtime Wages	Regular Wages	Overtime Wages
Membership Mgr.	9,000			
Asst. Mgr.	7,000			
Admin. Asst.	6,000			
Clerks	50,000	7,500		
Subtotals	$72,000	$7,500	$	$
Total Salaries	$79,500		$	

Salary increases in accordance with established guidelines.

	Actual Feb. 20X0 $1,003	Budget Feb. 20X1 $1,100
Travel		

Trip to Chicago, Ill., to attend membership marketing seminar.

Airfare = $500

Lodging = $600

	Actual Feb. 20X0 $5,308	Budget Feb. 20X1 $6,000
Printing		

Reprint membership recruitment brochure.

EXHIBIT 25.5 *(Continued)*		
	Actual Feb. 20X0	Budget Feb. 20X1
Postage	$4,156	$4,500

Bulk mail to send out brochure $4,000

Regular mail $500

	Actual Feb. 20X0	Budget Feb. 20X1
Supplies	$421	$500

Routine office supply purchases.

	Actual Feb. 20X0	Budget Feb. 20X1
Telephone	$491	$500

Local service $200

Long distance $300

	Actual Feb. 20X0	Budget Feb. 20X1
Miscellaneous	$485	$500

Unpredictable

EXHIBIT 25.5 *(Continued)*

Are there any expense items not listed that will be charged to the Membership Department in February 20X1? Explain and budget accordingly.

	Budget Feb. 20X1
Item: *Election*	$2,500

Print and mail bi-annual election ballots.

Printing = $2,000

Postage = $500

	Budget Feb. 20X1
Item:_____	$_____

_____

_____

_____

_____

_____

	Actual Feb. 20X0	**Budget Feb. 20X1**
Total Controllable Expenses	$83,247	$95,100

EXHIBIT 25.6

Sample Form for Inventory Purchase Request

Inventory Purchase Request
Membership Department
February 20X1

Name of Item   *Sweatshirts*
Intended Purchase Date: *February 20X1*

Costs:

Wholesaler	$1,600
Imprint Logo	200
Total Cash Required:	$1,800

Cost of Goods Sold Calculations

Total Cash Required *$1,800* ÷ Quantity Purchased *90* = Unit Cost of Goods Sold *$20*

Gross Profit per Unit

Selling Price per Unit *$30* − Unit Cost of Goods Sold *$20* = Gross Profit per Unit *$10*

Gross Profit Percentage

Gross Profit *$10* ÷ Selling Price *$30* = Gross Profit % *33.3%*

EXHIBIT 25.7

Sample Form for Capital Expenditure Request

Capital Expenditure Request
Membership Department
February 20X1

Item(s) Requested:

_____

Laser printer

_____

_____

Is equipment new _____ or replacement equipment _____✓_____?

If replacement equipment, describe old equipment:

_____

Dot matrix printer, serial 78930

_____

_____

_____

Intended purchase date: *February 20X1*

Anticipated Costs:

Equipment Cost	*$2,000*	Start-up Supplies	*$250*
Installation Costs	*$ 100*	Maintenance Contract	*$150*
Sales Tax	*$ 100*	Other Costs:	
Shipping Costs	*$ 50*	_____	____
Insurance on Shipping	*$ 50*	_____	____
Total	*$2,300*	Total	*$400*

Number of years equipment is expected to be used: *3*

FOR ACCOUNTING DEPARTMENT USE

EXHIBIT 25.8

Sample Form for Expense Reduction Plan

Expense Reduction Plan
Membership Department
Affected Month—February 20X1

The budget for your department is based on the assumption that revenues and expenses are realistic and attainable. Indicate your plan for a 5 percent reduction in the controllable and semi-controllable expenses charged to the Membership Department in the event that economic conditions force expense reductions.

1. Eliminate trip to membership marketing seminar.	$1,100
2. Reprint membership recruitment brochure in black and white instead of color.	2,000
3. Print election ballots in black and white instead of color.	500
4. Moratorium on office supply of brochures.	500
5. Moratorium on miscellaneous expenses.	500
6. Staff layoffs, salary freezes, etc.	10,000
Total	$14,600

Controllable expense budget	$95,100
Potential expense reductions	−14,600
Adjusted controllable expenses	$80,500

In a short amount of time, the membership manager of this association has done the following:

➢ Analyzed the actual revenue and controllable expenses for the month

➢ Submitted a brief report on the Membership Department's activities for the month

➢ Projected the budget for the same categories for the same month of the subsequent year

➢ Completed an inventory purchase request

➢ Compiled a capital expenditure request

Assuming the figures and explanations submitted to the chief staff executive were acceptable, the forms will be given to the budget coordinator, who will begin work on budgeting for the semi-controllable and fixed expenses for the Membership Department for the same month of the subsequent year. After this task has been completed, the budget coordinator will project cash flow for the period.

Because of the nature of semi-controllable and fixed expenses, the budget coordinator would most likely bypass the analysis of the current-month data form and proceed directly to subsequent-year budget projections (Exhibits 25.9 and 25.10).

After the membership manager's preliminary budget was approved by the chief staff executive, it was forwarded to the budget coordinator who projected the semi-controllable and fixed expenses for the Membership Department for the same period. Also taken into consideration was the Membership Department's effect on cash flow for the same month of the subsequent year, by including cash outlays for inventory purchases and capital equipment purchases.

The entire preliminary budget for the Membership Department, including the effect on each flow, may appear as shown in Exhibit 25.11.

EXHIBIT 25.9

Sample Form for Subsequent-Year Budget Projection for Budget Coordinator

Subsequent-Year Budget Projections
Semi-Controllable and Fixed Expenses
Membership Department
February 1, 20X1

	Actual Feb. 20X0	Budget Feb. 20X1
Fringe Benefits	$9,969	*$11,050*

Based on projected 13.9% of gross salary for fringe benefits in February 20X1.

$79,500 × 13.9% = $11,050

	Actual Feb. 20X0	Budget Feb. 20X1
Payroll Taxes	$6,686	*$7,393*

Based on projected 9.3% of gross salary for payroll taxes in February 20X1.

$79,500 × 9.3% = $7,393

	Actual Feb. 20X0	Budget Feb. 20X1
Utilities	$684	*$730*

Based on $1.50 per square foot realized in February 20X0 to $1.60 per square foot anticipated in February 20X1 for a 6.7% increase.

$684 × 1.067 = $730

EXHIBIT 25.9 *(Continued)*

	Actual Feb. 20X0	Budget Feb. 20X1
Other Taxes	$1,850	*$2,000*

Legislative approval of a .81% tax increase.

$1,850 × 1.081 = $2,000

	Actual Feb. 20X0	Budget Feb. 20X1
Rent	$5,000	*$5,500*

Lease escalation clause increases rent 10% effective January 20X1.

$5,000 × 1.1 = $5,500

Subsequent-Year Budget Projections
Semi-Controllable and Fixed Expenses
Membership Department
February 1, 20X1

	Actual Feb. 20X0	Budget Feb. 20X1
Lease Contracts	$570	*$570*

No projected changes in lease contracts.

	Actual Feb. 20X0	Budget Feb. 20X1
Semi-Controllable Expenses	*$19,189*	*$21,173*
Fixed Expenses	*$5,570*	*$6,070*

EXHIBIT 25.10

Sample Form for Subsequent-Year Cash Flow Projections

Subsequent-Year Cash Flow Projections
Membership Department
February 20X1

Cash Received:		
Dues and Affinity Credit Card Fees		+$301,250
Cash Disbursed:		
Controllable Expenses	$95,100	
Semi-Controllable Expenses	21,173	
Fixed Expenses	6,070	
Inventory Purchases	1,800	
Capital Purchases	2,700	−126,843
Net Effect on Cash Flow		+$174,407

EXHIBIT 25.11

Sample Preliminary Budget Form

Preliminary Budget
Membership Department
February 20X1

Revenues

Dues		$300,750
Affinity Credit Card Fees		500
Total Revenues		$301,250

Expenses

Controllable Expenses

Salaries	$79,500	
Travel	1,100	
Printing	6,000	
Postage	4,500	
Supplies	500	
Telephone	500	
Miscellaneous	500	
Election	2,500	95,100

Semi-Controllable Expenses

Fringe Benefits	$11,050	
Payroll Taxes	7,393	
Utilities	730	
Other Taxes	2,000	21,173

Fixed Expenses

Rent	$5,500	
Lease Contracts	570	6,070
		$122,343
Total Expenses		

Increase in Unrestricted Net Assets		$178,907

Other

Inventory Purchases	$1,800	
Capital Purchases	2,700	

Glossary

Accrual Accounting.   A system in which revenue is recognized when earned and expenses are recognized when incurred. Attempts to match revenue and expenses independently of cash receipts and disbursements.

Aged Statements.   A report breaking down the accounts receivable and accounts payable schedules into monthly categories based on the original date of the invoice.

Amortization.   Expensing an intangible or leasehold improvement over its useful life.

Assets.   Economic resources, including cash, receivables, property, and intangibles.

Audit Exceptions.   Problems incurred during the course of an audit by the independent CPA or the IRS.

Audited Financial Statements.   Financial statements audited by an independent CPA who has issued an accompanying opinion letter.

Balance Sheet.   See *Statement of Financial Position*.

Board-Designated Funds.   Amounts set aside by the board for a specific purpose that have no legal or accounting significance. See *Unrestricted Net Assets*.

Book Value.   The carrying value of an asset or liability, regardless of actual or market value. It is computed at cost less accumulated depreciation.

Capital Budget.   A budget that projects cash required to purchase fixed assets and resulting depreciation calculations.

Capital Lease.   A lease that is recorded as an asset and depreciated rather than expensed on the financial records as payments are made.

Capitalization.   Recording the costs of assets purchased on the organization's Statement of Financial Position rather than expensing them in the period purchased. Capitalized assets are depreciated.

Cash Accounting.   A system in which revenue is recognized as cash is received and expenses are recognized as cash is disbursed.

Cash Flow Budget.   A budget that projects cash available balances at the end of each month to ensure that enough cash is available to meet ongoing obligations to maximize investment.

Continuous Budgeting.   A process whereby monthly budgets are projected a year in advance every month after the current-period financial statements are prepared.

Cost of Goods Sold.   The actual cost of items sold to the organization that the organization intends to resell.

Credit.   An entry that results in a reduction in an asset account or an increase in a liability account.

Current Assets.   Cash plus cash equivalents plus assets that are expected to be converted to cash or consumed during the next 12 months.

Current Liabilities.   Obligations due to be paid during the next 12 months.

Current-Year Budget.   An organization's financial goals for the current year (also called tactical plan).

Debit.   An entry that results in an increase in an asset account or a reduction in a liability account.

Deferred Charge.   See *Prepaid Expenses.*

Deferred Revenue.   Revenue received before it is earned. It is recorded as a liability on the balance sheet.

Depreciation.   Expensing a tangible asset over its economic life.

Endowment Funds.   See *Permanently Restricted Net Assets.*

Expensing a Disbursement.   Recording a disbursement of cash as an expense in the financial records rather than capitalizing the disbursement and recording it as an asset in the financial records.

Financial Ratios.   Various computations to assess an organization's ability to pay debt, earning power, return on investment, and so forth.

Functional Accounting.   Classifying revenues and expenses according to specific goals, departments, functions, and so forth.

Generally Accepted Accounting Principles (GAAP).   A technical term encompassing conventions, rules, and procedures governing acceptable accounting practice.

Generally Accepted Auditing Standards (GAAS).   Assumptions and rules that govern the CPA's ability to accept an auditing engagement and procedure that must be undertaken during the course of the audit.

Gross Revenues.   The grand total of revenues received before deducting associated costs of goods sold and discounts taken.

Imprest Fund.   Also known as petty cash fund. Cash kept on hand to pay for minor expenditures.

Income Statement.   See *Statement of Activity.*

Intangible Asset.   A nonfinancial asset with economic value to an organization, for example, purchased copyrights with future royalty benefits.

Internal Financial Statement.   An unaudited financial statement used for management purposes only.

IRS Form 990.   Information return that not-for-profit organizations are required to file.

IRS Form 990-T.   Tax return that not-for-profit organizations are required to file for unrelated business income tax activities.

Leasehold Improvement.   An expenditure that improves leased property, such as the purchase of office carpeting. The value of the improvement transfers to the owner of the property after the lease terminates.

Liabilities.   Obligations to pay or to render services as a result of a past transaction.

Long-Range Plan.   An organization's goals for five or more years in the future (also called strategic plan).

Natural Accounting.   Classifying expenses as line items on financial statements rather than by function.

Net Assets.   Section of the Statement of Financial Position that includes unrestricted, temporarily restricted, and permanently restricted net assets.

Net Revenues.   Gross revenues less associated costs of goods sold and discounts taken.

Net Worth.   See *Unrestricted Net Assets.*

Operating Lease.   An ongoing-expense line-item lease. Operating lease expense is recognized on the financial statements as payments are made.

Permanently Restricted Net Assets.   Endowment funds and other funds that can be used only for activities stipulated by the donor.

Prepaid Expenses.   An expenditure incurred in one period whose benefits are not realized until a later accounting period (also known as deferred charges). It is recorded as an asset on the balance sheet.

Profit and Loss Statement.   See *Statement of Activity.*

Quid Pro Quo Contribution.   A contribution for which the donor receives some value in return.

Retirement of Assets.   Removing the cost and accumulated depreciation of an asset from the financial statements and records.

Statement of Activity.   Listing of revenues, expenses, and results of activities of not-for-profit organizations. Called income statement or profit and loss statement in commercial organizations.

Statement of Changes in Net Assets.   Financial statement of a not-for-profit organization indicating how results of operations have affected unrestricted net assets (net worth of the not-for-profit organization), temporarily restricted net assets, and permanently restricted net assets.

Statement of Financial Position.   Listing of assets, liabilities, and net assets of a not-for-profit organization. Called balance sheet in commercial organizations.

Strategic Plan.   See *Long-Range Plan.*

Tactical Plan.   See *Current-Year Budget.*

Temporarily Restricted Net Assets.   Results of fund-raising activities for a specific purpose or project.

Unrelated Business Income Tax.   Tax paid on profits from taxable activities. See *IRS Form 990-T.*

Unrestricted Net Assets.   The net worth of a not-for-profit organization, including board-designated funds.

Zero-Based Budgeting.   A system in which historical financial records are not used as a reference when budgets are prepared.

Index